Break the Binds of Weight Stigma

of related interest

The Ultimate Self-Esteem Toolkit
25 Tools to Boost Confidence, Achieve Goals, and Find Happiness
Risa Williams
Illustrated by Jennifer Whitney
ISBN 978 1 83997 474 8
eISBN 978 1 83997 475 5

The Eating Disorder Recovery Journal
Cara Lisette
Illustrated by Victoria Barron
Foreword by Emily David
ISBN 978 1 83997 085 6
eISBN 978 1 83997 086 3

Confronting Shame
How to Understand Your Shame and Gain Inner Freedom
Ilse Sand
Translated by Mark Kline
ISBN 978 1 83997 140 2
eISBN 978 1 83997 141 9

Unlock Your Resilience
Strategies for Dealing with Life's Challenges
Dr. Stephanie Azri
Foreword by Rachel Kelly
ISBN 978 1 78775 102 6
eISBN 978 1 78775 103 3

No Weigh!
A Teen's Guide to Positive Body Image, Food, and Emotional Wisdom
Signe Darpinian, Wendy Sterling and Shelley Aggarwal
Foreword by Connie Sobczak
ISBN 978 1 78592 825 3
eISBN 978 1 78450 946 0

BREAK THE BINDS OF WEIGHT STIGMA

Free Yourself from Body Image Struggles Using Acceptance and Commitment Therapy

DR. SARAH PEGRUM

Jessica Kingsley Publishers
London and Philadelphia

First published in Great Britain in 2024 by Jessica Kingsley Publishers
An imprint of John Murray Press

1

Front cover image source: Shutterstock®.

Disclaimer: The information contained in this book is not intended to replace the services of trained medical professionals or to be a substitute for medical advice. You are advised to consult a doctor on any matters relating to your health, and in particular on any matters that may require diagnosis or medical attention.

A CIP catalogue record for this title is available from the British Library and the Library of Congress

ISBN 978 1 83997 723 7
eISBN 978 1 83997 724 4

Printed and bound in the United States by Integrated Books International

Jessica Kingsley Publishers' policy is to use papers that are natural, renewable and recyclable products and made from wood grown in sustainable forests. The logging and manufacturing processes are expected to conform to the environmental regulations of the country of origin.

Jessica Kingsley Publishers
Carmelite House
50 Victoria Embankment
London EC4Y 0DZ

www.jkp.com

John Murray Press
Part of Hodder & Stoughton Ltd
An Hachette Company

To those lost along the way,
and those who carried me through.

Contents

Acknowledgements 11

Part One: The Forest

Introduction: Lost in the Forest 15

Chapter One: You Are Not to Blame for the Forest 21
Being human 21
The climate 23
A climate of weight bias, stigma, and discrimination 31
The human in the climate 32

Part Two: Preparation for the Journey

Chapter Two: Grab a Compass—Get Direction 37
Time machine 39
Who do I admire? 50
The body and values 53
Values lists and cards 54
Summary 55

Chapter Three: Charge Up 57
Prioritizing your values 59
Connect with you 60
No need to wait 62
Come back and recharge when you need to 64

Chapter Four: **My Forest** 65
Put on your glasses 65
Time machine to explore the beginning of trees in the forest 67
Awareness creates space for change 74

Part Three: Navigating My Forest for Me

Chapter Five: **Yes, the Forest Exists. No, You Can't Pretend That It Doesn't** 77
Avoidance of the painful body image trees 78
If struggling doesn't work, then stop struggling 85
Acceptance 87
Acceptance of the forest 89
Continuing in the forest 91

Chapter Six: **Take the Power Out of the Forest** 93
We think a lot 93
Fusion versus defusion 97

Chapter Seven: **My Emotions, My Signposts** 101
Exploring messages you received about emotions 102
What am I feeling? 103
I feel because I care 106
Take action to connect with what is important 111
Tools to keep moving in the face of the emotion 112
My own signposts? 114
Summary 116

Chapter Eight: **Change the Story** 117
My character: My story 118
Typecast 118
Breaking the typecast: Change the story 119
The story of you in the forest 122

Chapter Nine: **Correcting the Misguided Route to Belonging** 125
Fitting in versus belonging 125
Belonging from the inside 126
Small steps to being seen and creating connection 131
Summary 134

Chapter Ten:	**Get Moving!**	**135**
	A few things to remember before taking action	136
	Taking action	140
	Keep going	142
	Time for bigger change in the forest	144
Part Four:	**Navigating the Forest for Others**	
Chapter Eleven:	**Change the Dialogues**	**147**
	Micro acts of kindness	147
	Interrupting unhelpful acts	149
	Changing the dialogue at different levels	153
	Ripples in a pond	161
Chapter Twelve:	**Help the Youth**	**163**
	Help kids navigate the forest	163
	Work together to change the climate	168
	Changing the landscape takes time	173
Chapter Thirteen:	**Change the Climate at the Industry Level**	**175**
	Diet industry	175
	Fitness industry	179
	Fashion and clothing industry	182
	Social media industry	186
	A call to action	188
Endnotes		**189**
Subject Index		**197**
Author Index		**209**

Acknowledgements

While my name is on this book, it is hard to call it my own as it is a product of those who have touched my mind, my hands, and my heart. Those who have been researching, teaching, practicing, and sharing what they have learned. Those who have been battling the harshness of the world, had the determination to keep going, and the courage and vulnerability to share and let others into their experience. Those who inspired me and helped me persist even when the shadows of fear and doubt started to take over.

At the level of the mind, I'd like to acknowledge those within the Association for Contextual Behavioral Science Community (ACBS). Every time I have connection with this community, I learn so much and feel like I have a place where I can come out of hiding and am safe to be seen and heard. Much of the theory and the research within this book come from this community.

At the level of my hands, I'd like to thank my publisher, and all those who have helped with editing, and all the practical aspects of getting this book out there.

At the hands and heart level, I'd like to acknowledge those in the body acceptance, body positivity and fat activist movements. Many of you have experienced more oppression than what I can imagine, and yet in the face of this you have continued to carve out a path. A path that I hope more will walk on, but the path wouldn't exist if it wasn't for your fire, strength, and bravery. You are an inspiration to many.

At the heart level, I'd like to acknowledge all those who have been vulnerable, open, and shared their stories with me. For some it has been in the walls of therapy, while others it has been as colleagues, friends, or family. I'd like to thank those who were open to me sharing their experiences in this book. I feel my anger at the injustices of the world burn when I hear your stories. I hope that one day you, and the world around you, can see the incredible person I see in you.

Even closer to the heart, I'd like to acknowledge those in my inner circle who know of the struggles and losses I have faced whilst writing this book and have been there.

May this book be written and read now, so that it is in time no longer needed.

PART ONE

THE FOREST

INTRODUCTION

Lost in the Forest

I would like to begin this book with an image that came to mind when I first started writing: a forest. Not a magical beautiful forest, but rather a dense thick forest with trees and foliage that catch and tug at you, preventing you from freely moving around. The forest is an apt image to bring to mind when looking at body image, as just as the trees and vines in a forest can impair movement, our thoughts and feelings about our bodies can also impede our actions. We each have our own forest, where the trees and foliage are the thoughts and feelings we have about our bodies, and they impact how we move about in the world. Trees of "I can't do that until I lose weight," or "Only thin people can wear that," or "They probably wouldn't be interested in me because I'm fat," are all common body image trees in the forest. These trees can bring us to a complete halt on a path. You could be on the "I'm going to be more social" path, only to be brought to an abrupt standstill as you find yourself slamming into a "People will look at and judge me because of my weight" tree.

Alternatively, the trees may not stop us, but rather alter how we engage in our lives. For example, a person may go to a party wearing an outfit that is snug fitting and have a thought, "People will notice my stomach in this." The thought may not stop them from going to the party, but they may be self-conscious the whole night. They may possibly hold back or be less outgoing.

So, welcome to the forest. If you have picked up this book it is probably because you are feeling lost and stuck in the forest. Exhausted. Immobilized. Many people end up stuck here at some point in their lives. You are not the first, and I am sure you won't be the last, person to be lost in the forest. Maybe just as you are reading this book there is someone else reading it feeling the same way you do. You might not wish your struggles on anyone else, but there is something comforting in knowing you are not alone in the forest. It means you are not broken, but rather human, going through normal human experiences.

This forest is not of our making, though our minds like to tell us that it is. Our minds like to come up with a myriad of "what ifs," "if onlys," "shoulds," and "shouldn'ts," weaving a tale of how things could be different and creating a sense of personal responsibility for the forest.

Although our minds may try to sell us a different story, we are not dumb or superficial or shallow for being in the forest. Thoughts like, "You shouldn't worry about that," "That is so vain," "How shallow," or "That is superficial" may come rushing forward. Now we are getting hit twice: first by the pain created by being lost in the forest, and then by the pain created by self-judgment.

Just like the climate shapes the forests of the world, our forest and the trees within it have been nurtured and shaped over the years by forces in our environment. Environmental forces that have existed even prior to our birth. From a young age, you likely saw the climate forces and the trees and foliage, but may not have noticed them or their impact. It would be like asking a fish how the water is. It is so immersed in the water that it may not realize the temperature of the water, or why it swims in one area but not another. It is just there, and it just does.

Upon taking a moment and reflecting, you can see it, right from childhood. The laughter, the teasing, the bullying, the ostracizing of those who looked different. The subtle and not so subtle rules of who can do what and when, and who is attractive or accepted or successful, versus those condemned to just be there. To exist. Pushed into the shadows to not be seen or heard. All based on something as arbitrary as appearance. These experiences have given rise to the trees of how we think and feel about all aspects of our body. The trees of "I am not good enough, and I need to change."

The climate forces of the messages about appearance don't disappear as we move from childhood into adolescence, and then adulthood. Rather, messages about appearance just change as they get morphed by the rules of societal niceties and norms. Some overt comments a child may make are often not acceptable as an adult. New climate forces are added as we move towards sexual maturity and a new arena on which to be judged is brought into light. Thus, the forest continues to grow. A towering array of trees, a product of the internalization of all that is around us. Too fat. Too thin. Too masculine. Too feminine. Too short. Too tall. Too young. Too old. Skin is not the right color. Gender is not the right one. It can feel like there is no way to move forward or around without hitting one of these trees. The space left without trees creates a very narrow path of what you need to look like in order to succeed, be accepted and loved.

So, we may try to bend and contort to fit on that narrow path. Several big industries (such as cosmetics, fashion, and diet) thrive on the desire to find a path through the forest towards acceptance, belonging, success, and love. They claim to have the tools to help if you pay the price. Twist in this way and do this, and you will get away from those trees, and maybe the trees will disappear. But does that ever happen? Or does the twisting and contorting continue, yet the trees remain, leaving us exhausted, beaten down, and a shell of ourselves. We put so much of our energy into contorting, yet find ourselves in the same place. When we find ourselves in the same place after all that effort, do we blame the product, or the diet, or whatever it is we have tried to follow? Or do we blame ourselves for not being good enough? We don't think that the narrow path may be faulty. We assume we are the faulty ones.

Alternatively, we may respond to the forest by curling up and trying to shrink away from the trees. If people don't see or hear us, then our thoughts and feelings won't be confirmed by their judgments. The trees won't grow even bigger. Maybe we can just live out our existence in this safe, camouflaged, unseen state. If we are not seen, then others won't see that we aren't good enough. While it may feel protected, often this space is disconnected from the experiences and people that bring joy. Thus, we are in a bind: not happy in the shadows, but fearful to step out.

Either way, contort or shrink, it hurts. It hurts when we exhaust ourselves in pursuit of something that isn't true to us, only to find out it is still not enough. It hurts when we can't see who we want to be because the forest has taken over. Not knowing what is true to us and what is an internalized message. It hurts when we can see what is important to us but feel like we can't connect with it because of the forest.

Not only does it hurt us, but it also hurts the world around us. While we are contorting or shrinking, the world doesn't get to see the unique and amazing gifts that each and every one of us has. The world doesn't get to see the cracking wit, or the lightning quick intelligence, or the beautiful creativity, or the warmth of compassion, or all the other things that the forest blocks. So much potential and strength unseen and untapped. But what if it doesn't have to be like that? What if we don't have to contort to try and fit through the spaces of the forest? What if we don't have to curl up and shrink away? What if we don't have to wait for the trees to go away or change in order to move? What if we could look at the forest in a different way, and in doing so create space for movement and connection with who we want to be? What if by looking at the forest differently we can create change not only for us, but also for others who are trapped by the body image trees and stuck in the forest? What would happen if we unleashed not only our own potential, but helped others unleash theirs as well?

Break the Binds of Weight Stigma is about doing exactly that. Through the use of Acceptance and Commitment Therapy (ACT) it helps you accept that you may not be able to control the messages around you, or the thoughts that pop into your head, but you can change how you respond to them. You can take the power from those messages and thoughts and move your attention to taking action towards who you want to be and the life that you want to live. Yes, you are in the forest, but you can choose what action you take within it. That action doesn't have to be contorting, shrinking away, or waiting for the trees to go away.

In the following chapter we dive into the literature, exploring the brain and the societal forces that have led you and many others to getting stuck in the forest. You will see that you are truly not to blame for, nor are you alone in, the forest.

It can be overwhelming and daunting to think about the forest and how to navigate it differently. So Part Two is focused on helping you prepare for your journey by grabbing a compass, charging up, and learning about the terrain of your forest.

There are so many paths and possible directions for you to take in the forest, but not all the paths or directions will interest or excite you. Just because you can head in a direction doesn't mean it is a meaningful direction for you. Why put your time, energy, and attention into going towards something that doesn't excite you? In this section you will be introduced to exercises that help you identify what is important to you. What lights you up? Who do you want to be? What life do you want to live? The direction and energy gained from this section can help you throughout your journey, so it can be helpful to return to this section, particularly if you feel your motivation waver or lose sight of your direction. Just as you would consult a map or compass if you weren't sure if you were heading the right direction in a forest, you can return to these chapters.

Once you have worked out the direction you want to head, and have charged up, it is time to get to know the terrain of your forest; this part of the book will help you explore the different messages you have been exposed to throughout your life, and how they have impacted you. Understanding the broader climate, and your local climate, and how it has shaped your forest helps you navigate the thorny "Why?" or "I shouldn't think this way" trees and nurtures the "Ah, that makes sense" trees (which tend to be less thorny and have a comforting warmth to them). It also helps you identify which parts of the forest you find particularly difficult, and where you may really need some tools to help you move in the direction that excites you.

Once you have energy, direction, and know your terrain, it is time to experiment with navigating the forest differently, which is the focus of the third section of the book. Instead of contorting or curling up in reaction to the trees, you can take the power off the trees, and change how you respond to them. You can learn to effectively respond to the signposts of your emotions. You can become the hero(ine) of your own story. You can join with fellow travelers and feel like you belong. You can move through the forest towards being who you want to be and connecting with what is important to you. You no longer have to wait for your body to change in order to engage in life. Your body is not the problem.

Yet, you are not the only person lost in the forest, and more will continue to enter and get lost, unless action is taken at the climate level. Those things that you noticed shaping your forest are shaping other people's forests. Actions you take towards interrupting those forces could change the forest and help others be able to find their way. In the final chapters of *Break the Binds of Weight Stigma*, you can explore the various ways you can make a difference. Ways you can help other people shine.

ACT has been demonstrated as being effective not only in relation to body image, but also depression, anxiety, and behavior change. Thus, skills you learn to help you navigate the body image trees within your forest may also be helpful for navigating other trees and forests that may be in your life.

Break the Binds of Weight Stigma is not a book about how to lose weight, or how to get rid of those weight and body image thoughts. It is about helping you be more than just your weight. It is about moving society away from the importance of weight. We all have so much to give to those around us and the world, why should our value be minimized to a number on the scale?

A few things to remember as you go about your journey through the forest:

1. You are not alone in being here in the forest.
2. Being stuck in the forest is not a result of being a failure or being broken.
3. There are A LOT of things that have gone into creating the forest.
4. There are ways of navigating through or changing the forest landscape (if there weren't, the book would end here); and finally
5. Navigating through or changing the forest landscape can be done not only for you, but for those who are in the forest with you, and any people who may enter it in the future. We can draw them a map. We can cut them a path or build bridges over obstacles. We can be so much more.

Let us get going and take on that forest!

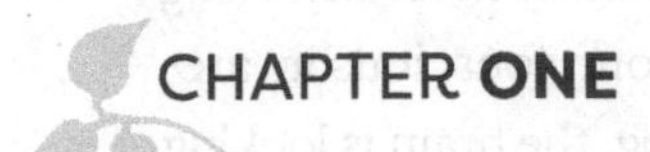

CHAPTER ONE

You Are Not to Blame for the Forest

Being lost in the forest is not your fault, and you are not alone in being lost. Your struggles are a product of being human in an environment that is highly appearance-focused. The society that we live in and the messages we have received throughout our lives have nurtured the body image trees that we are now pinned by. Furthermore, we, as humans, have incredible brains with processes that make us more alert to the social climate we live in, which further adds to the vulnerability to becoming trapped in the forest. Let us now take a moment to nerd out and look at how our brain and the climate have shaped getting stuck in the forest.

Being human

Humans are social mammals.[1] In ancestral times, our survival depended upon being in a group. In a group there is a sharing of resources such as food, water, and shelter. There is increased protection. One person may not be able to fend off a wild animal, but a group could. There is an increased chance of finding a mate and reproducing. Thus, belonging in a group is a basic need, and our brain has a variety of processes that facilitate social engagement to enable this need to be met.

These processes occur in the "newer" part of the brain. The newer parts of the brain tend to deal with social engagement and complex thinking (such as being able to use language and reasoning), whereas the older parts of the brain tend to deal with senses, movement, emotions, and instincts.[2,3] These newer parts of the brain interact with older parts. If we experience threats or safety in the newer part, the older part responds and allows us to take action.

Our brains are wired to notice social cues, particularly those involving the face and voice.[4] This noticing occurs without our conscious awareness. Before we have thought. At this level of noticing, the brain is looking at safety or threat. If a person is a threat, then I may need to activate the other instinctual processes to help me survive. If a person is deemed safe, I can override those other systems and move towards them with cues of safety so that we can work together.

Imagine being in an irritable mood. As you go about your day you come across someone who gives you an authentic, warm, welcoming smile, and speaks to you in a calm way. They show genuine interest and kindness. In this situation you may notice the irritability slightly dissipates. This is because your brain interpreted those facial expressions and vocal tone as safety, which then led to other brain and body changes.

Our brains are wired to quickly notice and respond to threats to basic survival needs. The need to belong is no exception. The pathways in the brain activated by the experience of being ostracized (threat to safety of being in a group) are the same pathways activated when experiencing physical pain.[5] Research has indicated that within 20 seconds our bodies can detect and react to ostracism.[6] As an example, you may walk into a room and get that gut feeling that you aren't welcome or don't belong. Your brain may not be getting any of those social cues that would activate the safety system.

Being human, we have the ability to communicate through language. Through language we learn and develop a complex web of how things relate to each other.[7] This can be helpful as it allows us to quickly learn, interact with the world, and make decisions. But sometimes strings in that web that we automatically learn, based on our experiences or observations, may not be accurate or helpful. In relation to the body, through language we may be taught and learn that a particular body type is good.

If you have ever played a word association game, you may have noticed that our brains are really good at exploding into all different directions of what is associated with a word. If you say the word "good" your mind will go to a whole array of things that it connects with "good." The brain has an incredible ability to deduce or make assumptions; if something is not in that pool of "good," then we assume it must be "bad." When you think of the word "bad," just like with "good," your brain can come up with all kinds of things associated with "bad."

As humans we are exposed to messages of what is a "good" body (we will go into detail on that in a moment). Our brain naturally inserts "good body" into the web of things associated with "good." It also creates the connection that if the body does not fit the parameters of "good" then it must be "bad." Those body types are then inserted into the associations with "bad."

When a person looks at their own body, they may put it in these learned language-based categories of "good" or "bad." This combines with the brain's miraculous ability to learn and form relations, and suddenly that which is associated with "good" or "bad" becomes attached to their body. For many, their mind may go a step further, not only labeling their body as "good" or "bad," but also who they are as a person. This thinking and interpretation layer may then interact with the instinctual need to belong (such as "If I am bad, then I will not belong"), which intensifies distress.

In summary, even before we start to look at the social climate we live in, you can see how as a human we are primed to notice and respond to social cues. The use of language further primes us to learn and create webs of how things relate to each other. This cognitive level of priming can contribute to an increased sense of threat, and thus distress.

The climate

We are going to take a moment now to look at the climate we live in, and how it has created and nurtured the body image trees so that they could take over the forest. To help capture living in the climate over time, I'd like to introduce you to Ava.

> Ava is the youngest of three kids in her family. She has an older brother and an older sister. She is a typical child, who likes doing what kids do. She looks up to her parents. Like most kids she at times watches them intensely, absorbing what they say and do, because she wants to be like them, and she wants them to love her.

> Her mum is always on a diet. Her weight is forever going up and down. The house goes through periods of time where certain foods are banished because they are "bad," but then they suddenly appear in abundance and Mum is back eating them until the next diet comes along. Sometimes when Ava brings treats home her mum cautions her, "You don't want to eat too much of that, or you will get fat," in a tone that implies being fat is the worst possible thing in the world to be.
>
> When watching her mum get ready to go out, Ava notices that her mum will try on a bunch of different clothes. Frequently bemoaning, "Urg, that one makes me look fat."
>
> As Ava grows, her clothes begin to get tighter. Her mum comments on this, "Didn't I just buy those pants? I don't recall them being that tight. You must have really gained some weight. We will have to keep an eye on you. Don't want you to get fat and unhealthy." Her father begins to make jokes, and her older brother chimes in.

So much learning takes place in the family environment that sets the foundation for future learning. The family unit provides information, directly and indirectly, about what is accepted and valued in society.[8, 9] As a result, the family can be a poignant source of information about the body, including what is associated with different body types (such as health), and what is valued (such as the thin/fit ideal). Many body and weight judgments and assumptions begin in the family environment.

Ava's story is not uncommon and is full of direct and indirect learning about body and weight. Indirect learning involves learning through observation, like Ava learning from watching her mum getting ready, making negative self-comments, and going on diets. These observations can set the norm of how to interact with one's body, and which bodies are valued or preferred.[10, 11]

Direct learning involves direct experience, such as Ava's experience of her mother making comments about Ava's food and body, and then her father and brother teasing her. One study found that nearly one quarter of middle school girls have experienced weight-related teasing from a parent (often the father), and one third experienced weight-related teasing by a sibling.[12] Parents engaging in teasing behavior acts as modeling, and siblings who have observed parents engaging in teasing are more likely to engage in teasing. Fathers and brothers are a source of information on what is important to the opposite sex and can act as models of interactions with the opposite sex.[13] Weight comments and teasing convey that weight is important, and that negative comments about the body are okay.

It is important to note that family interactions are a product of the family members' own experiences of societal climate, and their own forest. Some of the messaging in the family may be born out of parental exposure to messages about weight and health and may be coming from a protective place of wanting their children to be healthy.[14] Sadly, while weight-based talk and actions may be born out of concerns for health, they often have the opposite effect on a person's physical and mental health. Children from families where there was direct or indirect messaging in relation to weight tend to be more likely to have body dissatisfaction, low self-esteem, disordered eating, and eating disorders.[15, 16, 17, 18] These children also tend to struggle to engage in health-orientated activities (such as exercise for enjoyment) and are more likely to gain weight. These effects are not just observed while they are children, but also into adolescence and adulthood.[19]

> Ava turns on the TV. The shows are full of people who are thin or fit. A character appears that looks a little bit bigger than the others. Ava thinks the character's body looks more like how her body looks, and her attention is immediately drawn to them. Yet, they aren't on screen for long, and whenever they appear they seem to be laughed at. They are portrayed as lazy, dumb, and unhealthy.

From a young age, children are exposed to television. It gives them a glimpse of a world beyond or different to their family environment. Yet even in children's cartoons and shows there is an emphasis on the importance of physical appearance, as well as information about body and weight.[20, 21] The majority of characters are thin or "average" size, and those that are thin are often praised for their appearance.[22, 23] The few characters that are fat are often the source of comic relief. Moving outside of children's programming, into general programming, the theme continues—a lack of body diversity and when there is size diversity, the person who is larger is often portrayed in a negative light.[24, 25] In reality television, people who are larger are portrayed as needing to be fixed or transformed through weight loss so that they can engage in their life.[26,27] In recent years, there has been an increase in diversity on television, and increased portrayal of diverse sizes in a neutral or positive way. Hopefully, these changes are an indication of the beginning of broader shifts in the media's portrayal of the body.

> Ava goes to school. She likes to learn and read, and she used to love school because of this. But the kids are increasingly leaving her out of things. When they have to form groups for activities they go running to the other kids, and she feels left out. When she is placed in a group, the other kids in it look at her with disgust and disappointment. More recently, some of the kids make oinking and mooing sounds, and laugh at her at lunch and in gym class. As a result, she doesn't enjoy school as much, and is increasingly skipping classes or not going to school.

Peer interactions are where some of the messages learned from the family begin to play out beyond the family. It is also a place where new information can be gathered. Even by the tender age of three, children express preference for "thinner" or "average" size playmates, rather than fat playmates.[28] As children get older this preference manifests in the form of peer selection, rejection, and bullying, with the frequency and intensity increasing until it reaches its peak in the teen years.[29] At the level of peer selection many adolescents report that they would prefer to spend time with their thinner or "average" peers than their fat peers. Thinner or "average" sized kids are more likely to have friends, be included in activities, and seen as popular, while the kids who are fat are often excluded from activities and may have fewer friends.[30]

Not only are kids who are fat more likely to be excluded from social interactions with their peers, they are also at greater risk of being bullied than their thin or "average" sized peers.[31] Bullying can take a variety of forms, including teasing, name-calling, being ignored, threats, and physical harassment. Weight-related teasing is believed to be one of the most common forms of teasing.[32] By adolescence approximately 92 percent of kids have witnessed some form of weight-based teasing.[33]

Even if a child is not the victim of exclusion or bullying, they are impacted by it. They are noticing which kids are popular and included, and which ones are being excluded and bullied. They compare how their own body fits in relation to each. If their body is closer to that which is accepted, they may feel okay or good about their body, while if their body is closer to that which is rejected, they may feel dissatisfied, and want to change their body.

> What is helping Ava stay at school is her small group of friends. Her best friend Olivia frequently makes comments about her own weight saying that she is fat. The rest of the group assure her that she is not, yet the conversation makes Ava feel uncomfortable. She thinks, "If she considers herself to be fat, and she is smaller than me, then what does she think of me?" Ava's discomfort increases when she hears Olivia talking about how fat and ugly another girl is, and how she will never get a boyfriend because she is fat. Ava wonders if the same is being said of her when she is not around.

By adolescence not only are kids navigating differential treatment based on weight, but they are also increasingly being exposed to, and engaging in "fat talk." "Fat talk" involves a person making a negative comment about their body or size, such as "I feel so fat today."[34] The response to this often involves the other person also engaging in negative self-talk, and/or a reassurance that the person isn't fat.[35] While the reassurance that may occur in the "fat talk" may create the illusion that the talk doesn't have a negative impact on body image, "fat talk" is associated with increased body dissatisfaction, desire for thinness, as well as other eating disorder risk factors.[36, 37, 38] "Fat talk" draws attention to the importance of appearance and weight, and the desired standard. Women increasingly do not enjoy engaging in "fat talk," yet feel pressured to engage in it as it is perceived to be an expected part of social discourse.[39, 40] They feel like they should make such statements about their body. This is not all that surprising when one considers how common "fat talk" is. One study of US college women found that 93 percent engaged in "fat talk."[41] Another study of women from multiple countries, across a broad age range, suggested 81 percent of women engage in "fat talk" at least occasionally.[42]

Though "fat talk" may decrease moving further into adulthood, weight remains a regular topic of conversation. Comments are made directly to people about their weight. Often there is celebration of weight loss, and an assumption that it is an indicator of good health, hard work, and determination (unless it is an illness related loss). Weight gain is often met with negative comments, or suggestions of what can help to "fix" the problematic body. Even in a person's absence it is not unusual for their weight to be a topic of conversation, and assumptions are frequently made about what may have contributed to the weight change. For example, "Did you see how much weight she gained/lost?"

> Fast forward, and Ava is now out of school and a young adult. She has found a new group of friends who are far more accepting and supportive. Through them she found different people to follow and connect with on social media. They give her hope that she could one day, maybe, accept her body. Yet when she reads the comments on the influencers' posts, where people are calling the influencer fat and saying that they should cover up, she starts to think maybe she is just deluding herself and that the world will never accept her.

Most of us use some form of social media for a variety of reasons, including connecting with friends and loved ones, and finding communities where we feel like we belong. Social media is yet another avenue in which we learn what is the norm, what is liked, and what is not liked. Unlike magazines, movies, and TV that are full of models and celebrities, the people on our social media feeds are people we know, people we feel connected to, or people perceived as being like us. As social media is full of photos and videos it lends itself to being appearance-focused, and thus by its very nature conveys the message that appearance is important. But what appearances are preferred, and what are not preferred?

When we look at the general content of social media the predominant body shape is thin or fit. The sheer number of these images can lead to the assumption that this body shape is the norm or easy to obtain.

The portrayal of people who are fat, particularly on YouTube, is like that seen in movies and television, in that they are often portrayed as lazy, responsible for their weight, and are the target of humor.[43, 44] There are also high levels of weight-related shaming, teasing, and ridicule, and this content is often highly viewed and liked.[45] The fat body is portrayed as something that is not desired, should be avoided at all costs, and the individual is responsible for their size.

Social media is also full of "thinspiration" and "fitspiration" content, which is largely images of thin/lean people aimed at inspiring weight loss and fitness. "Thinspiration" has often been associated with promotion of a very unrealistic thin ideal and unhealthy means of achieving the ideal.[46] "Fitspiration" was initially seen as a healthier alternative to "thinspiration" as it was perceived to encourage healthy nutrition and fitness, as opposed to restriction and weight loss.[47] In more recent years, people have noticed a lot of similarities between the two forms of content.[48, 49] Both tend to predominantly contain an unrealistic thin ideal. Both tend to contain images that objectify women. Both often promote weight control behaviors. Both shame weight gain and being at a higher weight. It is like picking up a beauty or fashion magazine versus a fitness magazine; while the ideal may be slightly different for each of them, they both idealize smaller sizes, shame larger sizes, and portray weight as being controllable through diet and exercise. For many people, the effect of this content is that they feel more dissatisfied with and shameful of their body and are more likely to engage in unhealthy behaviors. Basically, they both make us feel uninspired and bad about our bodies.

There is an alternative to "thinspiration" and "fitspiration" content in the form of "body positivity," and "body acceptance." The "body positive" content encourages love and appreciation towards the body.[50, 51] "Body acceptance" content involves acceptance of the body regardless of whether one likes all aspects of it. Both "body positivity" and "body acceptance" promote the depiction and acceptance of bodies of all shapes, sizes, and abilities. The "body acceptance" and "body positivity" content is different to the "thinspiration" and "fitspiration" content in that it contains far more diversity of bodies, and often contains aspects of the body that are seen as flaws or as being outside of the beauty standards (such as cellulite, scars, wrinkles, and acne). The "body positive" and "body acceptance" content is also different in that there is far less encouragement to engage in weight control behaviors, far less body shaming, and far less objectification. While growing, the content is not as prolific as the "thinspiration" and "fitspiration" content.

The "body positivity" and "body acceptance" content appears to have a better impact on experience of one's body and mood compared to "thinspiration" and "fitspiration," in that many people report experiencing improved mood, body satisfaction, and body acceptance after viewing this form of content.[52]

The "body positivity" and "body acceptance" content has faced criticism (which is often evident in comments on postings), with some people suggesting that it encourages obesity and poor health.[53] This claim has yet to be supported by research.[54] In fact, research has demonstrated that when people feel positively towards their body, they are more likely to engage in health-promoting behaviors compared to when they are shamed or made to feel poorly about their body.

> Ava is interested in exploring her sexuality but is fearful of putting herself into the dating environment. She recalls the hurt of being left out in school, and the many times she was told that she wouldn't find a partner because she is fat.

In entering adulthood an extra layer is added for potential weight messages to play out, in the form of sexualization and intimacy. Dating and sex increasingly become topics of conversation, with a dominant theme that physical appearance and weight are important determinants of finding a person attractive.[55, 56] People who are thin or muscular are frequently perceived as attractive and are more likely to pursue dating or be in a relationship. People who are fat are perceived as less attractive and are less likely to date or be in a relationship. Exploration of common comments and interactions on dating websites and apps support these themes, with the presence of comments like "no fatties" on profiles or people screening out potential dates based on their size.

Weight-based comments do not cease upon entering a relationship. Many people report that their partner is a source of weight-based comments or teasing.[57] For women, weight-based comments often involve encouragement to lose weight. Partners with a significant difference in weight often encounter judgment, such as encouragement to keep the relationship and affection out of the public eye.[58]

> Ava has joined the workforce and prides herself on her work ethic. She is excited because she has just applied for a new position within the organization. The position matches her qualifications and experience perfectly. Her peers tell her that they can't imagine anyone else being a better fit.
>
> Ava doesn't hear anything about the position for a little while and she assumes that something may have come up that led to a delay in the hiring process. She later finds out that someone with significantly less qualifications and experience than her got the position. Through the grapevine she learns that despite having qualifications, experience, and great numbers on paper, the hiring manager perceived her as lazy.

Messages about body and weight are also evident in the workforce, and depending on where you work, they can be pretty overt, such as blatant comments about people's weight.[59, 60] Assumptions may be made about a person's motivation, engagement, and ability based on their weight, with people who are larger in size often being assumed to have less of a work ethic than their peers. Ava's experience is not unusual, and many people report experiencing weight-based discrimination or negativity in their workplace.

A climate of weight bias, stigma, and discrimination

The climate we live in is very vast, and the depiction of parts of the climate within Ava's story just scratches the surface. It doesn't even get into the underbelly of different industries (diet, fitness, beauty, fashion, health, and wellness), where messages are stronger and more rampant. This whole book could be completely dedicated to all the ways society impacts our perception and experience of our body.

What we see in Ava's story and when we look at the different parts of our climate, is a significant presence of weight bias, stigma, and discrimination. Weight bias is negative attitudes, judgments, and assumptions based on a person's weight.[61, 62] This is predominantly associated with people of higher weight, but people of low body weight also report experiencing negative assumptions and judgments. Weight stigma involves social stereotyping around weight and people who are fat. Weight discrimination involves treating people differently because of their weight. When someone has not had to face the struggles of weight bias, stigma, and discrimination, or has received benefits because of their size, they have experienced thin privilege.

Sadly, the presence of weight bias, stigma, and discrimination is rampant and has increased in recent decades. As evident in Ava's story, it has been observed in many different areas of life, and across the lifespan. Weight bias, stigma, and discrimination have a significant impact on people physically and psychologically. At a psychological level, people who have been victims of weight stigma and discrimination are more likely to struggle with anxiety, depression, eating disorders, substance abuse, and low self-esteem. At a physical level, exposure to stigma and discrimination activates the stress response system which impacts the immune, cardiovascular, and endocrine systems. Interestingly, many of the health issues associated with obesity are also associated with prolonged exposure to stigma and discrimination.

The human in the climate

> After this most recent hit from the workplace, on top of the others she has faced throughout her life, Ava sits beside you and cries. She hates her body. She sees her body and herself as "bad," "not good enough," "lazy," "worthless," "unhealthy," and "unlovable." You can't help but feel for her. Of course she would come to hate her body, after all she has been surrounded by and experienced.

Ava's brain is like yours and mine, primed to notice and respond to the social world around her. She has been surrounded by threat cues, and messages about "good" and "bad" bodies. Her body was deemed to fall in the "bad" category. In this context, what she is feeling and thinking makes sense. She isn't faulty or broken. Just like you aren't. Your brain is just doing what it is programmed to do, in a climate that contains vast messages of "thin/fit is good," and "fat is bad." The size and shape of your body can create a threat to your natural need to belong. The actions you might take, such as trying to change your body, or running and hiding, are actions born out of your mind trying to protect you from the threat. While these may be protective instincts, they aren't the most effective or helpful in the long term. These actions often lead to feeling less connected with yourself and with others.

Yet, you are not condemned to this struggle. The brain is incredibly complex, and it is possible to override the systems of language and threat detection. The skills covered in the chapters in Part Three of the book are tools to help you override the system, but before you can start to override responses, you need to have a reason why, as well as become aware of what responses need overriding, which takes us to the next section: preparation.

PART **TWO**

PREPARATION FOR THE JOURNEY

CHAPTER **TWO**

Grab a Compass— Get Direction

Reflecting on all the forces that have shaped the forest and the humans getting stuck in it can be very overwhelming. It can lead to thoughts of "Why bother? It is too big. I can't make a difference" or "I don't even know where to start." You are right. It is big, and at times it is hard to see and navigate the forest differently, and that is why it is important for you to have a "why" to your journey. The "why" helps give you direction. It can help you keep going even when the hard stuff appears, because the "why" is more important than the hard stuff.

The exploring of the "why" and establishing a direction can also be scary for some people. It's common to have thoughts like, "I don't know my 'why' or which direction to go," and "What if I choose the wrong 'why' or direction?" This may then be followed with self-judgment of "I should know!" It is okay. Many people don't know their "why" or direction. Often, we get caught up in the flow of life, following what we think we should be doing, and we don't take the time to think about why we are doing what we are doing. We get caught up in the problems in our life and what we don't want; we lose sight of what we do want and what is important to us.

This chapter is full of different exercises aimed to help explore and clarify a direction that feels like a fit for you. You may choose to do one exercise, or you may do all of them. From these exercises you may choose a direction, only to later realize it doesn't fit as well as you first thought. That is okay. Your path is not set in stone. People can change over time. You can always come back to these exercises and change your direction. Every direction will bring experience and learning. Even if the learning is, "I really don't like those experiences," it is still learning. You won't be the first, nor the last, person to pivot and change directions as information comes in.

One key directional tool on a journey is a compass. Using a compass, you can orient yourself to a particular direction, and throughout your journey you can keep checking back to see if you are still following that direction, as well as being able to identify and change direction as needed. You may head south for a period of time, and then decide that east is a better route for that moment.

Identifying your values is like creating your own personalized compass. Steven Hayes, one of the developers of Acceptance and Commitment Therapy (ACT), defines values as chosen qualities of action that people can work towards.[63] Values capture what is important to you, and who you want to be. They can be used to guide your actions. Examples of values include compassion, knowledge, adventure, openness, authenticity, creativity, freedom, fun, and independence. Values are ongoing, and "are more like directions in which one travels than destinations at which one arrives."[64] You don't achieve north, but you head north. Just like landmarks and destinations can be used to let you know you are still heading in a certain direction (for example, if I head east for 5km I will see a waterfall), you can set goals within your values that help let you know you are on the right path (for example, reading a book every two weeks may be a goal set under the value of knowledge).

Values can vary from domain to domain. Domains are the different areas of your life. What is important to you in the domain of relationships may not be as important in your work/career domain. For example, you may highly value honesty and loyalty in the relationships domain, but the importance of those values may dip in the work/career domain, and be replaced by other values, like productivity and achievement. This does not mean you don't value honesty and loyalty in the work/career domain, but rather the values of productivity and achievement may be more important in that domain.

Values can also change across the lifespan as your life changes. As a student in your 20s, you may have been inclined to value achievement, but in your 50s the value of compassion may overtake the value of achievement in order of importance.

As values can be dynamic and at times overwhelming, it can be helpful to choose a particular area to focus on and explore your values in that area first. Once you have explored that area, you can then move to other areas. Take a moment and identify areas or domains of your life that you would like to work on (such as family, work, leisure, or relationships).

Time machine

Our memories of the past and desires for the future can provide us with insight into our values. When we look at our past and see times that we were happy and content, it is likely that they were times that we felt connected to what is important to us. Conversely, the more painful memories are likely to be ones where we were disconnected from our values, or our values were threatened, or we lost something important to us. When we look to the future, the paths that we hope for and get excited about are likely ones that we feel put us closer to our values. The future paths we don't want, and fear, are ones that contain disconnection from, threats to, or loss within our values.

To help explore information on our values buried in our past, and in our desires for the future, we are going to enlist the help of a time machine. It is well beyond my scope of knowledge and experience to build a time machine like what you see in the movies and on television, but we all have a mental time machine. It is your brain's ability to replay memories from the past or imagine what could happen in the future. You may have used the time machine when feeling down and gone back over all the bad experiences you have had. Or you may have used the time machine when feeling anxious and jumped to the future trying to predict all the things that could go wrong.

In this book we are going to use the time machine a little bit differently from how you may have used it in the past. First, we are going to use it to gather information about what is meaningful and important to you. We are going to use emotions of happiness and sadness to guide the uncovering of values. If you are having an emotional reaction of happiness or sadness, chances are there is something (or multiple things) in that image that you care about in some way.

A number of worries can pop up for people even before they start playing around with the settings of the time machine. One cluster of common worries is "What if my time machine doesn't go anywhere or I don't find anything helpful in clarifying what is important to me?" That is okay. Not every exercise is helpful for every person all the time. There are so many different ways of uncovering values, so keep exploring and see what exercises are helpful for you. Also, sometimes in life it can be hard to identify values, for a variety of reasons. If you are struggling in your exploration, just notice what is coming up, be gentle with yourself, and reassure yourself that it is okay to be where you are right now. Remember you are not alone in being there.

Another cluster of worries that can come up when playing with the settings and going to different memories includes, "What if I pick the wrong memory?" or "It has to be perfect." Our time machines aren't like ones you see in the movies or television, where it is crucial that the characters go back to the exact right time and do the exact right thing. Our time machines are a lot more forgiving, and we can go back many times. There is not as much pressure. This is an information gathering exercise, so if you go somewhere (or go nowhere) that is all information that can help you.

Time Machine Setting: Past–Positive

Let us jump in the time machine. Set it to "past," and "happy," "content," or "true to self." Remember the memory you go to doesn't have to be perfect, or a big event, or one with intense feelings. It can just be a simple memory.

Let us return to where your time machine has taken you. The happy, true-to-yourself moment. Take a moment to think in detail about what was happening. Where were you? What were you doing? Who were you with? What was happening? What is it about this memory that resonates with you? What makes it important? What kind of person were you being? How was that shown in your actions? Build the picture in your mind. As you build the picture, and connect with it, do any feelings come up? Notice the feelings.

After you have spent some time building that picture up in your mind, it can be helpful to write down where you went in your time machine and what you noticed. You may have your own space to do this, or you could use the worksheet over the page.

If you want a guided audio version of this exercise, it is available at www.jkp.com/catalogue/book/9781839977237.

TIME MACHINE SETTING: PAST—POSITIVE

Identify a time in your life when you were happy or content:

....

....

....

....

....

What is it about this memory that makes you happy or content?

....

....

....

What kind of person are you in this memory? How are you behaving?

....

....

....

Does this memory point to anything that might be important to you?

....

....

....

Did any thoughts or feelings come up as you did that exercise?

....

....

....

Troubleshooting Time Machine: Past—Positive

The mind can come up with a lot of thoughts and feelings that create challenges in this exercise. If any of these blocks or struggles came up for you, you are not alone in that experience. You haven't done it wrong or failed. Different things help different people at different times.

- *"Am I doing it right?"* or *"What do other people get when they do this?"* I have done this exercise many times myself and with other people. One place my time machine goes is celebrating completing my PhD with my family. It points to some of the things that are important to me, like my family, connection, and learning. Other times I have gone in the time machine, and it goes back to time with my friends. Those memories stand out as they capture connection, fun, compassion, and authenticity.
- *"My weight was different then."* If your weight was different then, instead of focusing purely on that, notice what else was different other than weight. Did you act differently? How were your connections with others different? If someone was watching you then, what else would they notice is different?
- *"I was happy"* or *"I was confident."* For some people when they go back in their time machine, they focus on the internal things that were different. If those things come up, ask yourself, what did confident me do differently?
- *"I can't think of a really happy memory right now."* It is okay. Sometimes when we are in a rough place it can be hard to access those kinds of memories, and for some people life has just been mean and those glimmers are less frequent. It doesn't mean that will always be the case.

- *"I am so far from being that person I was in that memory."* This one can be tough and brings up some painful emotions. As hard as it is to see the distance between you now and who you used to be, in seeing it, you can change it. You can correct the course and get back. It is okay. Be gentle.

Time Machine Setting: Past—Negative

Before we move forward with this setting, I would like to give a warning: if you have a history of trauma or other very intense negative memories, you may choose to either skip this exercise or choose a memory that is milder in its intensity. The purpose of this exercise is to gather information, not re-traumatize you or push you into very intense emotions.

Often when we experience sadness it is because something important to us is being impacted negatively or threatened.

Jump in the time machine. Set the time machine to "past" and "sad." Where does your mind go? What makes that memory sad, is it that something you care about is being threatened or lost? Is it sad because you are not being true to what is important to you? What is creating the sadness? Explore and notice with gentleness and kindness.

As with the previous time machine exercise, once you have built the picture in your mind, it can be helpful to write down where your time machine went, and what you noticed. Again, there is a worksheet over the page that you can use to assist your reflection.

After doing that exercise, take a moment to be kind and compassionate to yourself. That may have been hard to look at. That took courage. It may have hurt. It sucks that the time machine has that place to go to, or many places like that. If you need to give yourself a hug or squeeze of the hand to warmly acknowledge the pain, do so. Remember that looking at some of this more painful stuff is in service of moving towards who you want to be.

A guided version of this activity can be found online at www.jkp.com/catalogue/book/9781839977237.

TIME MACHINE SETTING: PAST—NEGATIVE

Identify a time in your life when you felt sad:

. . . .

. . . .

. . . .

. . . .

. . . .

What is it about this memory that makes it sad?

. . . .

. . . .

. . . .

Does this memory point to anything that might be important to you?

. . . .

. . . .

. . . .

Did any thoughts or feelings come up as you did that exercise?

. . . .

. . . .

. . . .

Do you have any words of comfort you want to give that past you?

. . . .

. . . .

. . . .

Troubleshooting Time Machine: Past—Negative

Just as in the previous exercise, the mind can come up with a range of responses. It is okay. Notice what comes up with kindness and compassion.

- *"Am I doing it right?"* or *"What do other people get when they do this?"* One of the sad places that my time machine goes to is when my mother passed away from cancer. This memory hurts because it is a time when, not only did I lose someone I cared deeply about, but I also witnessed their suffering. The only way to completely get rid of that hurt and sadness would be to take away the care I have for my loved ones, and I would never trade that away. The sadness points to values I have in connecting with others.

  Other sad memories my time machine may go to are times when I was so caught up in my own stuff that I didn't listen to another person, I was rude, or at times downright mean. I didn't treat others with compassion or kindness, even at the most basic level. These memories hurt me, because they are times when my actions were very far from my values of kindness, understanding, and compassion.
- *Overwhelmed by the feelings attached to the memory or overwhelmed by the number of sad memories.* In looking at these memories it is important to do so with kindness and gentleness. Extend to yourself the kindness you would extend to others going through similar struggles. You are in the driver's seat with all these exercises. If they ever get too intense; stop. Breathe. Walk away from it and do something that soothes you.
- *"I can't find values in it. It is just sad."* Sometimes values don't jump out. It doesn't mean you have done the exercise wrong.
- *"What if I am destined to always be sad?"* Sometimes when we move towards feelings of sadness it can create a sense of permanency. This is often intensified by the time machine bouncing to all the other sad times. Step out of the time machine. Return to the present. Notice what is around you. Emotions come and go like waves. Just because you are feeling sad now, or have many sad memories, doesn't mean you will always be sad.

Time Machine Setting: Future—Positive

We are now going to change the setting on the time machine again, this time instead of going to the past, we are going to the future. A time in the future that you are celebrating an achievement, or maybe a birthday, and are reflecting back on what you have done. Take a moment to think of how many years in the future you would like to go. Some people set their time machine to many years in the future, others find that too overwhelming so set it to a time that is more manageable. Go with whatever speaks to you, there is no right or wrong, and you can always do the exercise multiple times.

Set the time machine to "future" and "celebration." Imagine yourself at a celebration. What are you celebrating? Where are you? Are you alone or are there people around you? Who is around you? What are they talking about? What is making you feel good or proud at that celebration? Continue to build the image and connect with the feelings. Notice if any feelings come up as you connect with the image.

Once you have created that picture, then take time to reflect and write down what you noticed.

For a guided version of this visit www.jkp.com/catalogue/book/9781839977237.

TIME MACHINE SETTING: FUTURE—POSITIVE

Describe being at a celebration in your future (for example, a birthday, achievement, retirement). What is the event? Who is there? What is being celebrated? What are things you have done or are doing? How does that make you feel?

....

....

....

....

....

....

....

Does this celebration point to anything that might be important to you, if so, what?

....

....

....

....

Did any thoughts or feelings come up as you did that exercise?

....

....

....

....

Troubleshooting Time Machine: Future—Positive

Just as with the previous exercises, the mind can come up with a range of responses. Notice what comes up with kindness and compassion.

- *"Am I doing it right?" or "What do other people get when they do this?"* Some people when they do the activity jump years and years ahead, and others have a shorter range. When I do this activity, I go to a time in the not-too-distant future (my time machine doesn't often go into long-range mode), and I am spending time with my family and I am sharing progress I have made with my business, places I have been, and people I have seen. I am happy, not only because I am connecting with my family, but also because I am helping people. It brings up domains of family and work, and values of connection and helping others.

- *"I don't know if I will ever be able to do that."* That is okay. Remember this is just information gathering, finding out what may be important to you. You are not committing to anything. Be gentle.
- *"What I was celebrating is not possible."* That can really hurt. Acknowledge the pain or feelings that come up. One of the things I enjoy about values is that even if they can't be achieved in the way that you initially stumble on them, there is often another way of accessing them. Try to move away from the specific content and see if you can see values hidden within it.
- *"I can't think of anything."* That is okay. Not all these exercises are helpful for everyone all of the time. Sometimes during times of uncertainty, it can be hard to set the time machine to "future." Again, be gentle.
- *"My mind goes to more macro or global struggles (such as climate change)."* It is hard to go to the future when there are some of those big picture things that can significantly impact what the future looks like. If your mind goes to those places, who do you want to be in the face of those big picture struggles? How would you be handling it that would make you feel proud?

Time Machine Setting: Future—Negative

Last time jumping in the time machine for now. This time we are going to the future again, but this time nothing in your life has changed or maybe it has gotten worse. Again, set your machine to whatever time in the future suits you.

Jump in the time machine, set the machine to "future" and "no change" or "gotten worse." Where does the time machine go? What is happening? What are you doing? How are you spending your time? How are you feeling? Is there anyone around you, if so, who?

Once you have created that picture, then take time to reflect and write down what you noticed.

For a guided audio version of this go to www.jkp.com/catalogue/book/9781839977237.

TIME MACHINE SETTING: FUTURE—NEGATIVE

Describe a future where things haven't changed or have gotten worse. Where are you? What is happening? Who (if anyone) is around you? What are you doing? What thoughts and feelings are you having?

Does this future draw your attention to anything that might be important to you, if so, what?

Did any thoughts or feelings come up as you did that exercise?

Troubleshooting Time Machine: Future—Negative

Just as with the previous exercises, the mind can come up with a range of responses. Notice what comes up with kindness and compassion.

- *"Am I doing it right?" or "What do other people get when they do this?"* Honestly, out of all the time machine exercises, this one is one where my machine doesn't give as clear a picture as the others. It goes to a time in the not-too-distant future (like I said before, the long-range setting doesn't come up much on my machine) and I am bored and in a rut. The list of "things I would like to do" has the same stuff I have on it now, plus more, and I am less able to do them. I feel like I have failed, and my time is running out. I feel listless, worthless, disconnected, and frustrated with myself. This future me is very distant from values of openness to experiences and connection.
- *"My mind goes to more macro or global struggles (such as climate change)."* As I mentioned in the last troubleshooting section, it is hard to go to the future when there are some of those big picture things that can significantly impact what the future looks like. It may be helpful to change your time machine setting, so it isn't as far into the future (maybe just one or two years).
- *Emotions.* Sometimes when people go into their time machine in this setting it can bring up intense emotions, including that of sadness or anxiety. Breathe. Be gentle. This is all information that can help you. This future is not set in stone, and there may be things you can do to help shape it.
- *"I can't think of anything."* That is okay. Not all these exercises are helpful for everyone all the time. Sometimes during times of uncertainty, it can be hard to set the time machine to "future." Again, be gentle.

Who do I admire?

We are now going to leave the time machine and the focus on the self alone for a little bit, and we will instead turn our attention to the people we admire. We tend to admire people because they possess qualities we value and may want ourselves. Thus, in looking around at the people you admire, you can gather further information about who you want to be. Your mind may push back and say, "I could never be like them." Remember, this is just gathering information about what you value. Later we will look more at refining the list of what is important to you and determining steps you can take.

Take a moment. Bring to mind someone you admire. They could be someone close to you like a family member, or friend, or colleague. Or they could be someone you don't know personally, but who you admire, like a sports star or celebrity. What is it about them that you admire? How do they approach the world? How do they approach other people? How do they approach difficulties? What makes them stand out to you?

Again, take a moment to reflect and write down what came to mind.

For me, I consider myself lucky in that there are many people in my life whom I admire for a variety of reasons. In my personal life, my parents each had qualities that I admire, and I am happy when I see myself connecting with those qualities and values (such as wisdom, adventurousness, strength, openness, humor, and compassion). In my professional life I have also encountered people that I admire for their wealth of knowledge, courage, kindness, and compassion.

WHO DO I ADMIRE?

Who do you admire?

....

....

....

....

....

....

....

Write down all the things you admire about them.

Are there things you admire in them that you want to strive to be, if so, what?

The body and values

In the appearance-focused world that we live in, a lot of things get attached to body and weight. As a result, at times when we are pursuing an ideal (or running from a not-ideal) it isn't just about the body. It is about what we believe will happen upon moving towards or away from the ideal. In this next exercise, we explore what has become attached to the ideal body and not-ideal body and see if they are connected to the things that are important to you.

Take a piece of paper, on one side write body ideal in a bubble, and then on the other write not-ideal body in a bubble. Alternatively, on the worksheet over the page you will find two bubbles. One stating BODY IDEAL and another, stating NOT-IDEAL BODY. Take a moment to bring each image to mind (the ideal and not-ideal body), and notice what you associate with each of them. Write those associations in the space next to the appropriate bubble. For example, some people associate being popular, in control or healthy with the ideal, and lazy, unhealthy, unpopular with the not-ideal body.

A lot of the time when people are talking about body image and their struggles, they have thoughts that they are being vain or superficial. When you look at your worksheet, and you cover the bubble of BODY IDEAL or NOT-IDEAL BODY, is the stuff that remains superficial or is it connected to some of your values (such as values of connection, health, productivity)?

ASSOCIATIONS WITH THE IDEAL AND NOT-IDEAL

BODY IDEAL

NOT-IDEAL BODY

Values lists and cards

If these activities didn't speak to you, which is very possible, especially if you are not someone whose brain likes visualization and who tends to do better with recognition tasks, don't panic. This does not mean that you are someone who doesn't have values or doesn't find anything important or meaningful. There are resources online that you might find useful.

Try searching for "values lists" or "value cards." These search terms give a big list of different values and common definitions attached to them (though you can always attach your own definition).

Summary

What have we done in this chapter: we have explored memories, looked into the future, looked to those we admire, and looked at what we attach to the body. These explorations help uncover values by bringing attention to what is important to us. These values can then be used to set a direction, just like points on a compass.

Still confused? That is okay. Maybe a lot came up for you in the exercises and you are confused and overwhelmed, or maybe very little came up and you aren't sure what your values are. Whatever your experience is, it is okay. Values are something you can always circle back to, and we return to the topic throughout this book. Just like on a journey you can check back to your compass to work out which direction you are heading.

CHAPTER **THREE**

Charge Up

Just like you would charge your phone and any other electronic devices before you go on a trek, this chapter is about doing that for you: charging up and getting motivated. Just as you may need to recharge your phone or electronic device during a journey, you may need to return to this chapter to recharge and get motivated again.

I'm going to begin this chapter with a story. At first you may think, what on earth does this have to do with anything, but bear with me, keep reading and hopefully it will weave together.

> In 2019, I was very fortunate to be able to go to Uganda, an incredibly beautiful country in Eastern Africa. My partner and I hold similar values (including adventure, curiosity, and openness to the different experiences in the world), so when planning the trip, we had thoughts on all the different things we could do and see. One thing that we both agreed would be a "must do" on our trip was gorilla trekking, and we made sure it was in our itinerary. Gorilla trekking is a form of eco-tourism, and the funds raised go back to conservation of the gorillas.
>
> The gorillas in Uganda are mountain gorillas, not gentle hill gorillas or flat plain gorillas. Mountain gorillas, so to get to them, you need to trek up a mountain. A mountain that is very steep in parts. We naïvely over-estimated our capabilities and under-estimated the terrain and didn't think we would need hiking poles. It wasn't far into the trek that the guides insisted on hiking poles and cut us some from the forest. I am so grateful for that, as who knows what state our bodies would have been in had it not been for the poles.
>
> The mountain gorillas are located in an area known as the Bwindi

Impenetrable Forest, again very aptly named. We had to follow our guides who were hacking a path with machetes, but even with them hacking away, the forest felt impenetrable. The forest was so dense. I have never seen anything like it. There were so many vines that would trip and entangle us and others in our group. If the vines didn't entrap us, the other trees and plants covered in thorns would hook us, pulling us to an abrupt halt. At times we would simultaneously get hooked by and tangled in the vines and thorns. The instinct was often to try to pull through to get out of the vines and thorns with brute force, but that was wasted energy and we would still be stuck, or our clothes torn to shreds. The more effective strategy was to move slowly and carefully, noticing what had brought us to a halt (vine, thorn, something else) and respond accordingly: slowly unhooking or untangling ourselves or getting a fellow trekker to help us.

Some people who do gorilla trekking find their gorillas in an hour. Not our group. I recall times when both my partner and I would get tangled and stumble. We would curse, and you could see the frustration and exhaustion in our faces. Were there moments where we wished we were not there? Yes. Were there times where we would think "argh, not again!" as we tumbled or got hooked? Yes. Were there moments where we thought about turning back, and that we made the wrong decision in doing this? These moments were briefer, but yes, those thoughts came up as well. Were there times where we would beat up on ourselves and doubt our capabilities? Absolutely. It was hard. It was exhausting. It was, at times, absolutely defeating.

After over two hours of trekking up a mountain, and through the impenetrable forest, we found our gorilla family. We saw a 13-year-old gorilla, holding her firstborn baby, only a few months old. He was so small, and his fur on his head was so thick and long that it puffed out. The interaction between mother and baby was so human-like. She seemed to look at him with such tenderness. The little one was curious about these new human arrivals and kept looking over and wanted to move in our direction. The mother scooped him up in her arms and lumbered towards us, before sitting again. They were now much closer to us. Both she and the baby made eye contact with us, a mutual curiosity. Words cannot describe how I felt in that moment. In that moment, all the struggle, frustration and exhaustion that had been present just moments ago in trekking through the impenetrable forest seemed to take a back seat, and in its place was this incredible moment of magic. A once in a lifetime experience. An experience so few will ever have.

It rained on the way back down the mountain, adding yet another layer of treachery to the trek. We were by far the last group of trekkers to return to the station and were soaked with both rainwater and sweat. Altogether we were trekking the mountain for approximately seven hours. Was it hard? Was it exhausting? Were there times I doubted what I was doing on that mountain? Absolutely. But was it worth it to get those magical moments? One thousand times yes, yes, yes. As someone who values adventure, curiosity, openness, and seeing beauty in the natural world, that was a moment that will forever stay with me, and the struggle was 100 percent worth it.

Why tell this story? Because looking at your forest and navigating through it may sometimes be really hard and really exhausting. Your forest may feel like an impenetrable forest, with vines and thorns constantly tripping and hooking you. Yet, if trekking through the forest is in service of your own gorilla moment, then you will feel like the struggles were worth it. In looking at your values, like you did in the last chapter, you were gathering clues to what might make your gorilla moment. What will make the struggles worthwhile?

Prioritizing your values

When my partner and I were planning our trip to Africa we wanted to see everything, but it just wasn't possible. We had to prioritize what we wanted to see and do in the time we had. Values can be similar. When looking at a list of values, it can be tempting to select nearly all of them as being important to you. Yet just like it wasn't possible for us to see and do everything in Africa, it isn't possible to hold all values, in all domains, at all times. Like prioritizing experiences on a trip, prioritizing values is a way of prioritizing what kinds of experiences you want in your life, whatever the timeline is.

Reflect on the exercises from the previous chapter and write down what emerged as your values or what is important to you. Once you have compiled your list, begin to group them in order of importance. Place the three or four values that are most important on the top tier, others that are important can go on the second tier, and any values remaining can go on the third tier.

You may experience different thoughts and feelings as you move the values to the different tiers. Notice these thoughts and feelings, and what may be driving them. For example, you may really value creativity, but those around you may not, and as a result you may feel anxious about putting creativity on the top tier, or sad if you move it to the bottom tier.

Remember, values can always be moved from tier to tier. Different domains or situations may call for the movement of values. Hence, try not to stress too much about which tier a value is on; it can always change. This is all learning, exploring, and trying things on.

Connect with you

Now that you have your top tier, we are going to take a moment to really connect with your values and charge up. Get in a comfortable position and close your eyes. Take a few breaths to centre yourself, and then bring to mind those three or four values. Imagine being someone who embodies those qualities. Imagine being that you, who you want to be. Where is that person? How do they carry themselves? How do they sit or stand? If you can, sit in that position, really connecting with that part of you. What are they doing? How would other people know they hold those values? Really build a detailed picture of what it would look and feel like to be living true to those values. If any thoughts or emotions pop up as you do the exercise, just notice them, and return to connecting to that image of you being the you that you want to be. With each breath in, connect with what it would be like. Then when you are ready, bring your attention back to the here and now. Begin with what you can feel: your feet on the floor, the chair underneath you. Then move your attention to what you can hear. When you feel ready, open your eyes and take in what is around you.

For a guided version of this exercise go to www.jkp.com/catalogue/book/9781839977237.

After doing the connection exercise, take a moment to write down what you noticed in the experience; noticing what you connected with, and how your mind reacted to connecting with you, the person you want to be.

You can access that version of you at any time by doing that connection exercise, but there are other ways to connect with that part of you. You may choose to name that version of you, such as future me, or adventurous me, or badass me.

For a number of years, I was a skater, coach, and referee in roller derby. For those unfamiliar with roller derby, many people in roller derby come up with a derby name. Mine was Tassie Devil, as I had recently moved from Tasmania, Australia to Canada. For some, having a derby name created an alter ego. Often it gave them an opportunity to explore or try on different aspects of self. For example, a person who is very shy and timid in their regular life would have a derby persona of confidence and having a voice. Interestingly, over the years I observed that for several skaters, elements of their derby persona started to creep into other areas of their life. Being part of roller derby and having a derby name created space and allowed people to connect with a part of themselves that they were disconnected from, and it then grew. Labeling that version of you can have a similar effect, allowing you to create space and try on that version of you and see if you want it to grow.

Another way to connect with the you that you want to be is through posture and positioning. When you think about that version of you, how do they sit or stand? For example, a strong or courageous you might sit and stand upright with shoulders back, ready and able to take on the world. If there is an identifiable stance or posture, move yourself into that posture to connect.

Does that you have a particular taste in music or sounds that they like? If so, surround yourself with those sounds or that music. Create your own charge up or connection playlist. My charge up playlist has a lot of music by the artist P!nk. When I am feeling vulnerable and scared and am wanting to connect with my values of courage and strength, I put on my playlist. The fear and vulnerability doesn't go away, but I feel stronger in the face of it and more able to act.

Are there other things attached to the you that you want to be, such as smells, tactile sensations, or clothing? If there is anything that you attach to that you then surround yourself with it, particularly when you are wanting to be that you. Each time you connect with this part of you, you are practicing being you, and you are forming new pathways in the brain. Over time these pathways get stronger, and you move from practicing or behaving as if you are that person, to actually being and doing.

No need to wait

Returning to the story of the gorillas: when we were looking at all the options of things we could do on our trip, we could have easily removed the gorilla trek for a variety of reasons: physical ability to climb the mountain, time it takes to get to the area where the gorillas are found, or expense. If we didn't think we were physically able to climb, could get to the location of the gorillas, and be able to afford the experience, we wouldn't have put it on our itinerary. Instead, it would have gone on the list of "cool things we would like to do but can't." So, let us now take some time to build a sense of hope and possibility.

Take a moment. Think about a role that you hold that is important to you. It could be your role as a parent, child, sibling, partner, friend, or employer/ee. Choose a role. Then take a moment to think about what is key to making a person good in that role. What makes a good parent, child, sibling, partner, friend or employer/ee? Write it down, either in a place you have created, or on the worksheet over the page.

If you are struggling to come up with ideas it may be helpful to think of someone you know, or have seen, that you admire, and think about what they do that makes you appreciate their approach to the role.

Once you have completed the list, look back over it. Is weight on the list? Are any of those things on the list completely weight-dependent? Or can you take steps towards being those things on the list regardless of your weight? Life isn't like those rides you see at an amusement park stating you have to be within a particular height or weight range to participate. You can participate now.

WHAT MAKES A GOOD ....?

Take a moment. Think about a role that you hold that is important to you. It could be your role as a parent, child, sibling, partner, friend, or employer/ee. Choose a role. Then take a moment to think about what is key to making a person good in that role. What makes a good parent, child, sibling, partner, friend or employer/ee? Write what comes to mind in the space below.

....

....

....

....

....

....

....

....

....

Notice if any of the qualities noted above are appearance or weight dependent, or are you able to connect with them regardless of your weight. Note any thoughts that come to mind as you reflect on your list, and whether or not qualities on your list are weight dependent.

....

....

....

....

....

....

....

One of the many things I like about doing values work is that often, no matter what is happening with your weight or life, you can usually find some small step to connect with your values. For example, if you value compassion, you can be compassionate to yourself and to other people no matter what your weight is. There is no one standing around saying that a compassionate act doesn't count because your weight is above or below a certain number. Regardless of your weight (as any weight is okay), you can take steps right now towards connecting with your values and being the person you want to be, which is really cool.

Come back and recharge when you need to

Just like the batteries on our electronic devices run low, and we need to return to our chargers and recharge them, you may also find your energy and motivation may get depleted and need recharging. In a world where you are bombarded with weight-related messages, you may find your batteries run out of juice and need recharging often. If at any point you begin to waver, and your battery needs charging on the journey, come back to this chapter and charge up again. You deserve to be living your life according to what is important to you, and you can take steps towards that, regardless of what your weight is.

CHAPTER **FOUR**

My Forest

By now you have an idea of the climate forces that shape the forest, and you have your "why" giving you your direction and charge. It is now time to look at the local climate and how it has shaped your forest. Looking at our own experiences can bring up a range of thoughts and feelings that can then obscure our vision and blind us. Like looking into the sun. Before proceeding forward in this self-reflection journey, I encourage you to put on your glasses. Not sunglasses or reading glasses, but glasses of compassion and curiosity.

Note: if you have trauma or abuse in your history I would not advise digging too deeply in this chapter's exercises without the help of a professional, as it could bring up some very intense emotions and memories.

Put on your glasses

In the years of working in the field, whether it is talking with people struggling with an eating disorder, body image, or just in general, I have heard many people get frustrated with themselves and the way their mind is responding: "Urg! It is just weight. I shouldn't be letting it get to me. This is so superficial and vain." I have also fallen into that frustration when catching myself going into a negative spiral: "I work in this field. I should know better." It adds to the sting that already exists. Yet as we saw in Ava's story, the feelings and the thoughts are not about "just weight." The struggles are about the experience of carrying the body around in the world and all the interactions that come with it.

When we reflect on the experiences of our past that shaped body image struggles, it is not unusual for judgments towards our younger self to emerge. Judgments of how our younger self thought, felt, and behaved. Thoughts of "I can't believe I did that," "I should/shouldn't have..." or "How stupid or naïve was I?!" Feelings of guilt, shame, disgust, and sadness. Thoughts, feelings, and judgments of those around us and their actions may also emerge. Blame, and thoughts like, "Who says that to a child?!," "That was so mean," or "They didn't care about me" may appear. As may feelings of frustration and anger.

We can get lost in these thoughts and feelings and become blind to why we are looking at these past experiences. We are looking at these experiences, not to blame or shame, but to help understand how the trees in your forest grew. To ease the shame and blame, and to introduce compassion and validation. To see which body image trees may be particularly big or pervasive. The ones we may need the most help with. To help take the power off the forest, so we can more freely move around and be true to who we want to be.

Remember, our brains are programmed to notice and respond to the social environment around us, as this helps us connect with others and belong in a group. The environment we are attuned to is *full* of messages about weight and body. Our struggles are not about "just weight." The struggles are about being hurt or feeling vulnerable to being hurt. No one likes to feel judged. No one likes to be looked at with disgust or spoken to in a condescending way. It makes sense to want to protect yourself from that experience. Actions taken were likely a form of protection. The actions may have involved shrinking away to not be seen or heard. A run to safety. The actions may have involved lashing out, pushing other people away, pushing them down to feel better about oneself. Fight to safety. The actions may have involved desperate attempts to fix one's body to fit what is deemed "good." Fight to safety. Looking back now, knowing what you know, you may not like or agree with what you or those around you did, but in the context of being a human in an appearance-focused world, the actions make sense. You were doing the best you could with what you had and knew, as were those around you.

I encourage you to hold onto this lens as we walk through and investigate the forest, and throughout this book. A lens of "It makes sense I feel this way or react this way, when this is what I have been exposed to," instead of "I should or shouldn't think that way." Looking at your past in this way doesn't take the pain away, but through this lens there is a little more compassion and kindness.

Yet, compassion is only one part of your glasses' lens, another part is curiosity. Imagine watching two episodes of a show: one is a repeat of an episode you have seen before, and the other is a new episode. Which of the episodes would you be more alert in? Which episode would you be more curious about?

When we are in new environments or doing new things we tend to be more alert, and to notice what is around us. We absorb more information. We don't have as much previous experience shaping assumptions and narrowing our vision. When we look at our past, we can do so in the same way that we would approach the repeat episode. We may notice some things that we didn't notice the first time, but chances are we aren't as alert, and our mind is jumping ahead and filling in what we know is going to happen next. Alternatively, we can approach looking at our past similarly to how we approach the second or new episode, with curiosity. Thoughts of "I wonder what is going to happen next..." or "Oh, that is interesting." Through the lens of curiosity, we let go of the grip of previously held ideas, and instead we view things as if we are seeing them for the first time, with an air of wonder.

Wearing the glasses of compassion and curiosity, you are less vulnerable to the glare of shaming and blaming that can occur when examining the forest.

Time machine to explore the beginning of trees in the forest

With compassion and curiosity glasses on, let us jump back into the time machine. This time we are putting the settings to "past" and "messages about weight and body." You may notice your time machine trying to search for the best, most salient, most impactful memory. Or you may notice it races to a whole heap of memories, so many that you can't pick just one. Just notice and observe where your time machine goes. It doesn't have to be the best or most salient memory. Just memories of things that impacted how you feel and think about your body and weight. As you watch these memories, think about what message they convey about body and weight. What did you learn?

When I step into my time machine and go to "past" and "messages about weight and body," I get a montage of weight-related comments, fat jokes, and people making fun of people who are larger. The montage begins with my family, and times when family members would make jokes and laugh at my mother, who was bigger. As my attention expands out beyond the family, I get images of family friends doing the same to Mum. The montage continues, now showing me images of people at school, again fat jokes, thin/fit being praised or adored, and fat people being laughed at or playing the role of class clown. Television and media also make a brief appearance in the montage. Fat characters being the ones that bring comic relief, and the use of fat suits to exaggerate the stereotype and get more of a laugh. There is a strong theme of "fat is bad," and that "people connect through weight-related comments and jokes."

Staying in your time machine and with the memories. Notice how those experiences made you feel. Notice how it impacted your thoughts and the actions you took back then. Also notice the thoughts and feelings you are having right now as you look at those memories.

When I go in my time machine and view the montage a range of emotions emerge. I notice that as a child I felt conflicted. I was close to my mother. I felt uncomfortable with the comments being made. I wanted to protect her and stop them. I was also the youngest in the family. I wanted to connect with members of my family and feel like I belonged. I went along with the jokes and didn't say anything. I notice that this pattern continues with the other memories, particularly if the person being commented on or teased is closer to me. Those in the media or at a distance seem to be dehumanized, and the discomfort is lessened, and it is more about entertainment or connection. I notice as I look at the memories and experiences that guilt, shame, and self-judgment arise towards the not taking action, yet compassion also arises for the part of me that wanted to.

Those experiences were in the past. Did the messages and learning from those experiences stay in the past, or did they carry with you throughout your life, and continue to impact you today? Take a moment to think if those learnings stayed with you, and how they have impacted you over the years and in recent times.

My learning that "fat is bad" and "connect through weight comments and teasing" continued throughout my life, in part because experiences that conveyed these messages kept happening around me. The teasing and commenting on people's weight didn't stop when I reached adulthood. It wasn't something that kids and teenagers do, but adults don't because they grow out of it and have learned better ways. No. It was still there, and as noted in the previous chapter, an extra domain was put forward for these messages to play out, in the form of desirability and intimacy.

The "fat is bad" learning had me fearing weight gain. Growing up I wasn't thin, but I wasn't fat either. I was average. Attention wasn't given for my body being good or bad. I could hide and be safe from being seen and judged. I recall losing weight due to illness when I was 17 years old, which of course was praised. When I was 18 years old I started to gain it back, and I recall being worried about seeing the number on the scale go up. If I gain weight people will notice. They will judge. They will make comments. They will laugh at me. They won't like me. They will reject me. I will be cast aside. Alone.

Fast forward to the present day. I don't weigh myself. I like to be active, but don't have a body that captures that. During times of stress, injury, and inactivity I have gained weight. Even after research and working in the field of eating disorders and body image for over 15 years, those old thoughts and fears creep in. Don't get fat. What will people think? What will they say? They will think you are lazy, unhealthy, and worthless, and you are.

The impact of "connect through weight comments and teasing" learning on me in my life makes me cringe. As a result of this message and learning my actions, or often more inaction, have run smack against my values and what is important to me. When people have made weight-related comments or jokes there have been many times where I either did nothing to interrupt it, or worse, went along with it. This brings guilt and shame. The conflict that I recall experiencing as a child witnessing comments to my mother, and later to my peers, kept resurfacing. Feeling for the person who the comment or joke is directed to and wanting to stand up and say something to interrupt, yet also fearing what would happen if I did. If I say something, how will people respond? Will they turn on me? Will they laugh at or attack me? Will they reject me? At times I did stand up and say something, and this resulted in me being laughed at, teased, and yes, pushed away. So, I would return to being silent.

Over the years I have connected with my values and found my voice more and more. I don't want to connect through comments and weight-related teasing. I don't want to belong where that is considered okay, and if that means that I am standing alone or get rejected then so be it. I can't be a part of it, and I can't stand by and not take action anymore. I don't engage in weight-related comments, jokes, or teasing. I aim to interrupt it when I see it. Writing this book is a step towards interrupting it. Yet even as I write it, that fear is there. You are going to be a target now. People will turn on you. Be quiet. Shut up. Go back to being unseen. You are safer there. Someone else can take that on.

Yet my experiences come from a place of thin privilege, and so my words only capture a portion of what can be experienced as a child, youth, or adult. People who have bigger bodies than mine didn't have the privileges that I had, and have a different experience when they jump into their time machine. Here are just a few experiences from people around the world:

> The first time I remember a comment on my body sinking deeply in me and making me feel hurt was when I was about seven or eight years old. I was doing the fitting of the tunic for my first communion and the nun dressing me told how I would need something to contain that pop belly. I've had similar comments made throughout my life, but that was the first that I remembered feeling complete and utter shame. Those words always affected me the way I looked and perceived my body, the clothes I chose, how the t-shirts always need to be longer, the dresses not too fitted in that part. Still, it does affect me at some stages but much less then it used to. (Francesca, Italy)

> After I dislocated my knee at netball, I visited my Nana who said, "Well you'd have to expect a person carrying extra weight to injure themselves." I was in a healthy weight range. Additionally, I grew up with very active parents who both feel I'd be happier if I shifted my weight and felt better about the way I look. They would tell me to exercise more (even though they knew of my knee injuries and back pain, and that prior to that had been doing high intensity workouts five to six days a week), and to eat

> less (even though I was calculating my intake in accordance with my activity levels). So I was eating within my calories but being told to eat less. (Michelle, Australia)

Some people receive "compliments" whereby some positive attribute would be noted, only to be ripped away by a weight reference, like "You look so pretty, imagine how stunning you would be if you lost weight."

> A comment from a friend of my mom, was that I was such a lovely girl. So smart. So driven, independent and everything. If only I was just a bit skinnier. Then I could find love and have everything else going even better for me. (Francesca, Italy)

The different generations have their own experiences that shape their relationship with food and body, which can create challenging interactions, particularly when they are different to our own experiences and growth.

> I was 21 years old and on a surprise visit to my grandparents. My grandmother had been a model in the 40s and 50s and had lost her first husband in the immediate World War 2 aftermath. Meanwhile, I had a history of disordered eating in high school (mostly restricting and purging). I had since learned about feminism and started a feminist body image website. My numbing behaviors had shifted to binge eating after a death in the family a year before this visit. After I had been there for about 20 minutes, my grandmother and I were alone in the kitchen for a minute. She said, "You've put on some weight there, gal." I smiled brightly and said, "I have, thanks for noticing!" Later, once we all gathered in the living room, my grandmother said, "So who's been making all the lasagna at your house?" Puzzled, I said, "Sorry, lasagna?" In reply she said, "I'm just teasing you about all that weight you've put on." I smiled again. "I've been reading about our beauty standards, and I think they're disgusting. Only 4% of women can fit that oppressive weight standard." My aunt stepped in and said, "I've gained some curves since I started eating meat again, and I like them." It was my grandmother's turn to be puzzled. (Nikki, USA)

It is not just the comments and actions of others that can send us messages about our bodies, but also the environment itself.

> I had to get accommodations because I often don't fit in the seats used in exam rooms. I would scope out classrooms at the beginning of the semester and drop/add classes based on the style of desk/chairs. I've always seen this as a me problem, and it is me who has to change. It is only as I approach my 40s that I am starting to be kind enough to myself to understand that I deserve space too. (Cindy, Canada)

Into adulthood, the comments and actions continue, not just from loved ones, but also those in positions of power, like medical or health care professionals. The weight discrimination encountered can not only impact how we feel about our bodies, but also about our health and our lives.

> My intense menstrual pain was written off for ages, claiming if I lost weight, it would improve. I lost the weight they mentioned. I admit I went to extreme lengths to lose weight which has led me to have a very complicated relationship with food that lasts until this day. After the weight loss I still had the pain. Only at that point was I approved for testing, which inevitably lead to my diagnosis of uterine and ovarian cancer. I had a hysterectomy. My heart hurts, and I mourn the fact that I can't have a child with my new husband. I blamed myself for so long, that if I managed my weight after having my kids I could have been diagnosed earlier and still have children now. (Melissa, Canada)

I've shared some of my experiences, and those of others around the world, to help you on your own self-reflection journey. To further assist your exploration, I have included a guided reflection exercise, which can be found at www.jkp.com/catalogue/book/9781839977237. Over the page you will also find a table to organize your thoughts and reflections, and for those who like to journal there are reflection question prompts.

INFLUENCE OF MESSAGES AROUND BODY AND WEIGHT

Time machine setting	Experience	Messages and learning	Influence: Thoughts, feelings, and actions as a result of the experiences
For example, "past-childhood/teens," and "messages about weight."	Family and family friends teasing Mum who was larger, peers connecting over fat jokes at school, media portrayal of fat characters as comic relief.	Fat is bad. Weight-related comments, jokes, or teasing is a way to connect with others.	Fear weight gain and associated negative social perceptions and reactions with it. Conflicted—felt for Mum and others receiving comments and jokes but didn't feel like I could stand up or say anything as that would threaten connection and belonging. As a result, I would go along with what the social norm was. Guilt and shame for actions and inactions taken or not taken.

SELF-REFLECTION QUESTIONS: HOW MY FOREST SHAPED ME

- What messages did you receive about shape and weight throughout your life?
- How were those messages conveyed?
- How did you feel, and what thoughts did you have when those messages were being conveyed?
- How did the messages you received impact your actions at the time?
- Did those messages stay in the past, or did they continue to influence you?
- How did those messages continue to influence you? How have they impacted your thoughts, feelings, and actions?
- Are there any thoughts and feelings emerging as you do this reflection and look at your past self? If so, what?
- Is there anything getting in the way of being able to view these experiences through the lens of compassion and curiosity? If so, what?

Awareness creates space for change

It isn't comfortable to look at this stuff, and that is why it is important for you to keep your compassionate and curious glasses on, to help ease that pain that can emerge. Going into the time machine and going back to the past can also sap you of your energy. Yet as painful and energy draining looking at the past pain can be, in looking at the difficult stuff you are starting to take the power off it. You are building awareness, which creates space to learn how to make different choices in the future. Choices that will help you connect with what is important to you. Choices that help you interrupt these messages in society and help others.

PART THREE

NAVIGATING MY FOREST FOR ME

CHAPTER **FIVE**

Yes, the Forest Exists. No, You Can't Pretend That It Doesn't

Reflections emerging from the previous chapter may have brought forth a range of emotions; some of them may have been particularly uncomfortable. The uncomfortable emotions may be regarding how you feel about your body, or they could be regarding how you responded to or acted on the messages around you.

Humans, like most animals, don't like to feel uncomfortable, and will do what they can to try to avoid discomfort. There are two common pathways we use to get away from pain and discomfort. One path involves trying to struggle, fight, or fix what is perceived as causing the pain. In this response we are tackling what we believe is the problem and trying to make it go away. In many areas of our lives this active responding doesn't cause problems and is even helpful. If it is raining outside and you don't want to get wet, but you need to go out, you avoid the discomfort of getting wet in the rain by getting an umbrella or raincoat. Problem fixed; discomfort averted.

When it comes to emotions and internal experiences, this way of responding is less effective, especially when it is our only way of responding. There are probably multiple times in your life when you have been distressed, and there is nothing you can do to fix what is causing that distress. Grief and loss are such examples; you feel sad because you have lost someone, and you can't bring the person back. You cannot make the distress go away by fixing the problem.

The other default response style is avoiding by running, hiding, or blocking. Again, it makes sense for the brain to turn to avoidance, as it is a response that has probably been effective in the past. If being around cats makes you sick because you are allergic to them, an effective way of not getting sick would be to avoid cats.

However, just like the fix it/problem-solve response, the avoidance response style is more challenging when applied to thoughts or emotions. Some common ways people avoid thoughts and feelings include distractions, sleeping, keeping busy, not going places or seeing people, trying not to think about distressing things, or using drugs or alcohol. Avoidance can sometimes be helpful or necessary as it can buy us time or allow us to have a break. Yet, when it is used all the time or is the only way we respond to pain or discomfort, it becomes problematic.

While these are the two most common ways that people respond to discomfort, there are other ways of responding. In this chapter, we will first look further at how you respond to your forest, the pain it creates, and the impact of the responses. We then begin to explore an alternate way of responding.

Avoidance of the painful body image trees

Given the pain that the climate and our body image trees can cause, it makes sense that we want to avoid it, either by fixing or running and hiding. But the forest is a part of us and a product of the climate we live in, and as a result these efforts are often limited in their effectiveness and/or have a hefty price tag attached to them.

Below is a list of common responses to uncomfortable thoughts and feelings about weight and body. Take a moment to look through the list and notice if you turned to any of these responses to navigate your body image trees.

- Exercise.
- Diet.
- Surgery.
- Weight loss drugs.
- Not looking in the mirror or at your reflection.

- Spend a significant amount of time trying to find an outfit that fits or looks right.
- Spend a significant amount of time trying to get hair and make-up to look right.
- Avoid looking at yourself when naked in the bath or shower.
- Turn lights off when being intimate out of concerns that the other will see.
- Avoid certain clothing (such as tight or revealing clothing).
- Avoid places or activities (such as the beach or running).
- Avoid interacting with people.
- Avoid having photos taken or avoid looking at photos.
- Avoid being the centre of attention.
- Eat, over-eat, or binge eat.
- Alcohol.
- Cannabis.
- Cigarettes.
- Other substances.
- Watching TV or movies or things online.
- Scrolling on social media.
- Keeping busy.
- Other: ....

The actions on the list capture two default styles of responding: fix it/problem-solve or avoid.

Fix it or problem-solve

The first response style of fix it/problem-solve involves trying to get rid of the thoughts or discomfort by fixing the problem identified. Underlying this response style is the assumption that once the supposed problem is fixed, the uncomfortable thoughts and feelings will go away. Based on the messages we receive in our climate, what we identify as being the problem is the body and, more specifically, weight. There is an assumption that upon losing weight things will improve. Statements like, "Once I lose weight, I will feel better," or "Once I lose weight, I will be able to date" capture this pattern of thinking.

As weight is identified as the problem, many people then throw their attention and energy into fixing it via exercise, diet, weight-loss drugs, or surgery. The path this takes for each person can vary. Many people, particularly those who throw their energy into strict dieting in an effort to fix the problem, find that despite their efforts to fix the problem, the problem remains. The weight and the uncomfortable thoughts and feelings are still there. This brings on another series of uncomfortable thoughts and feelings, such as feelings of disappointment and thoughts of "It is not working," or "I am failing." In response to this discomfort a person may give up their exercise or diet plan and spiral into further difficult thoughts and feelings (such as shame or guilt). Alternatively, they may vow to do more and try harder, and throw more attention and energy into their efforts to fix their body.

Unfortunately, there are several industries that make money from this path of responding. While they may be associated with weight loss in the short term, many ways that are touted as quickly solving the weight problem (such as strict diet, pills) are not sustainable, and often result in people regaining lost weight, plus some more. When this occurs it is the person who is blamed and shamed, rather than the diet, pill, or exercise plan. This leaves the door open for the person to hand over more money to recommit to what they were trying or to try something new. Newsflash: It is *not* you; it is them.

Others who have thrown their attention and energy into fixing the problem find that they have lost weight, but the uncomfortable thoughts remain. This is confusing; if weight was the problem and it is gone, then why are the thoughts and feelings still here? This may lead to thoughts of "Maybe I just need to lose a little more, and then the thoughts will go away." As a result, they continue with, or increase, their efforts to fix their body. They may find that each time they achieve their goal weight the uncomfortable thoughts and feelings remain. They then set a new goal in the hope that the discomfort will disappear when the new goal is achieved.

With each of these paths, the energy and efforts to fix the body are often at the expense of other things in a person's life. Despite the time, energy, and attention directed towards getting rid of the discomfort by fixing the problem of weight, the uncomfortable thoughts and feelings remain, and for many they become more intense. Thus, what begins as a protective path attempting to move a person out of harm's way, actually ends up causing more harm.

Avoid it

The second response style of avoidance can take several forms. It may involve trying to avoid anything that draws attention to the body, because that in turn evokes negative thoughts and feelings. Many people avoid certain people or gatherings of people due to fears of comments or judgments about their body, or they may go but hold back as they don't want to draw attention to themselves. They notice initially experiencing relief as they are not having to navigate social situations and judgments, but often this is followed by a sense of missing out and disconnection. Over time the more they avoid social situations they start to receive fewer and fewer invites, and they feel more alone. The comfort initially felt from choosing to be alone on occasion turns to distress as the alone time feels less like a choice.

> I limit my Facebook and Instagram profiles to select people so on the off chance I post a photo of me, anyone who knew the old me wouldn't see it. I also avoid shopping (do mostly online), or even just going out for meals, to the beach etc. In the off chance I see someone I know, I don't want to be the topic of their conversation: "Have you seen how fat Michelle has gotten?!?!" (Michelle, Australia)

My go-to response is avoiding by running, hiding, or blocking. As a child I remember playing a game called Spotlight; it was a game played at night. There was a central spot identified as "home" (when we played in my yard it was a tree). One person was designated as being "it." They would go and count while everyone else hid. The person who was "it" had a flashlight, and they would "tag" people out by shining their light on them. The goal was to get to home, where you would be safe. People would try to find a good hiding place so they wouldn't be spotted right away, and then try to find a way to either sneak or sprint home before being spotted by the person who was "it." Basically, if you weren't seen you would be safe. I took this premise out of the game and into my life. If I wasn't the centre of attention, I wouldn't be spotted and would remain safe. My avoidance.

The hiding brought me a sense of safety, but it severely limited my sense of connection with other people. If people can't see you, they can't connect with you. So, while I felt safe, I also felt alone. When life events happened (both good and bad), I felt isolated and sad.

Many people avoid activities where their bodies are more exposed (such as swimming) because they make them feel vulnerable. If it is an activity that a person doesn't enjoy that much, or isn't a significant part of their life, this may not cause distress. However, if it is something they enjoy, or that is a part of their life, or a way of connecting with others, the distress associated with avoidance increases. Many parents have expressed feelings of sadness that they are missing out on time playing with their children due to their own discomfort with swimming or physical activity.

Clothing selection can be another way of avoiding or hiding one's body. Many prefer loose fitting clothing, certain styles or patterns that hide parts of their body they are uncomfortable with.

> I've always had an athletic build. When my partner and I got together he said, "With calves like those, you should be pushing barrows." I was always self conscious about my muscley athletic build. After that I barely wore short dresses and hate wearing shorts, opting for pants, maxi dresses or long skirts. (Michelle, Australia)

Sometimes these clothing decisions come from the well intended recommendations of family members.

> My family, in their own strange way to protect me, they always told me to hide that part of my body, stand up straight, suck it in, wear an under shirt or contention body shaper. (Francesca, Italy)

Being alone with the body can be very challenging for many, and they may struggle when looking in the mirror or having baths as they are visually confronted with their body. Many people report having challenges with intimate relationships as they struggle with their own naked body, and the thought of someone they love seeing and judging it. This can impede the progression and enjoyment of intimacy with their partner.

Another form of avoidance involves trying to avoid or block the uncomfortable thoughts and feelings about the body. Many people report feeling uncomfortable in their own skin and have a desire to get away from this experience. They may turn to distraction (such as watching television, scrolling, keeping busy) or numbing out (such as drinking, drugs, eating) to get away from their internal experiences.

> Drinking booze is an issue. I have become so uncomfortable in myself that I just want to drink. When I feel left out or not good enough in social situations, I drink more and more to get my confidence up, and kinda force myself to be extroverted so people would want to get to know me. (Michelle, Australia)

While watching TV or scrolling through social media may initially keep the uncomfortable thoughts and feelings at bay, they generally don't build a sense of achievement or mastery, or even relaxation or rejuvenation. As a result, many feel like time has passed but they have nothing to show for it, or feel listless, stuck, or like they are just punching their time, existing.

Distracting oneself by keeping busy can create a sense of achievement, as you check items off the "to do" list. It is often socially reinforced as well, with people providing compliments about how much you do. It can be an alluring form of avoidance. Yet, while one's attention is focused on keeping busy, it is pulled away from noticing the body and emotions. As a result, body cues and emotions that may indicate that one is pushing oneself too much or too far may get missed. It is not unusual for people who avoid by keeping busy to report experiencing a physical or mental breaking point forcing them to slow down or stop. At the time it feels like it has come out of the blue, but as they heal and look back, they often see that there may have been warning signs that were ignored. A person in hindsight may see that they were tired or more prone to illness, signs that the body was running on empty, but they only stopped upon becoming significantly ill. In hindsight, they may see that they were a little more irritable, or not as bubbly as they previously were, but only slowed or stopped upon having a severe panic attack, angry outburst, or depressive episode.

Whether responding with fixing it or avoiding it, there is a pattern of some initial relief or reward. However, over time, as the response is at the expense of other things in a person's life, it becomes less helpful and creates more distress.

SELF-REFLECTION EXERCISE: WHAT PATH DO I TAKE?

Some of these paths (fixing or avoidance) may seem familiar to you, or you may have your own path. Take a moment and think about which path(s) you have tried. Then ask yourself the following questions.

- What uncomfortable thoughts and feelings led me down this path? For example, felt uncomfortable in my clothes, was worried that someone would comment on my weight, or had gained weight.
- What do I feel when I am on this path (both initially and over time)? For example, initially I felt really good, like I was finally doing something about it. But I just couldn't stick with it. It was so frustrating and disheartening to constantly be trying over and over again.
- How do I feel about myself as I continue down that path (initially and over time)? For example, I felt like a failure, lazy, and there must be something wrong with me. Why can't I just keep at it?!
- How connected am I to my values and what is important to me when I am on that path? For example, I spent a lot less time with my friends and family, and when I was with them, I was lost in my head thinking about exercise and food. So, I guess I was less connected to my values of connection and compassion.

Those questions can be pretty confronting, as they can bring to light the extent of time and energy that has gone towards something that hasn't brought you any closer to who you want to be. Some people experience a variety of thoughts and feelings as they complete the exercise, including a sense of grief over the loss of time, guilt, shame, frustration, or anger.

If any of these feelings emerge, it is normal. If they don't emerge, that is normal too.

Both fixing it and avoiding responses involve struggling with the forest. Yet the forest took a long time to grow and is weaved into many of your memories and experiences. Therefore, struggling with it takes a lot of energy, and often the thoughts and feelings remain, and may even increase. Added to that is that while you have been struggling with the forest time has passed, and you may be further from the you that you want to be.

If struggling doesn't work, then stop struggling

If trying to get rid of the discomfort via struggling with it by using fix it or avoidance doesn't bring you closer to your values, then let go of the struggle. This sounds simple, but in practice is very challenging. If it wasn't challenging, you would have done it already.

The first step in letting go of the struggle involves noticing when you respond in ways that move you away from your values. With this awareness in hand, the next time you start to feel an urge to respond in the fix it or avoid way, use the urge as a marker for you to pause. Ask yourself, "Am I entering into the struggle?" and, "Will this pull me away from my values?"

If the answer to those questions is "yes," you may want to extend the pause a little longer. Continue to breathe. Move your mouth towards a soft, closed mouth with a relaxed partial smile. Acknowledge what is present that has activated the urge to struggle, as if you are greeting a casual acquaintance, "I see you shame. I see you 'I am fat' thought. I see you disgust." You don't have to do anything with what you see. You don't have to like it or agree with it. You are letting go of putting your resources into struggling with it to make it go away. You are just letting it be.

Once you have acknowledged and made a little space for what activated the struggle and the urges to enter the struggle, you can explore what action you could take. Ask yourself, what response would be consistent with my values and what is important to me?

I have wanted to write this book for years. I could say that I didn't start to make a genuine effort on it because I was too busy with work and other things in life. Yet that is a story I have told myself to justify or rationalize not taking steps. In being honest with myself, not writing this book was a way I could stay in my hiding space. In writing a book, I am stepping out of my hiding space. I am in the wide open where the spotlight can land on me. It is scary. Yet staying in my hiding space wasn't consistent with who I want to be. I want to connect with people. I want to be open to life experiences. I want to help and empower others. When the fears and urges to hide come up, I see them. I let them be and continue to step out of the hiding space. This is not easy, and there have been many times where I have had to turn to others to help me do it.

GUIDED EXERCISE: ACKNOWLEDGE

Take a moment. Close your eyes. Sit in a comfortable position. Gently draw your attention to your breath. You don't have to change it. Just observe it. Settle into this moment. Move your mouth to a relaxed, gentle, closed mouth with a partial smile.

Imagine you are in front of a mirror, looking at yourself in it. Notice all the usual thoughts and feelings that would come up with doing that activity. Take a moment. Breathe.

Imagine those thoughts being like a child or animal peeking out from behind a tree. Turn towards them. Compassionately and kindly acknowledge their presence. Maybe with a little head nod like you are greeting an acquaintance. "I see you. I see you shame. I see you disgust. I see you, 'You can't go out like that' thought. I see you, 'You are fat' thought." Breathe. In acknowledging that you see them, you are giving them permission to come out from behind the tree, and to just be there. If the thoughts are racing or the feelings are clumped together, label that and see that too, "I see you racing not good enough thought. I see you tangled bundle of emotions." Breathe. Let the thoughts and feelings be. You don't have to like them. You don't have to agree with them. You are simply letting them be. Other thoughts and feelings may emerge as you acknowledge the presence of these thoughts and feelings. Acknowledge them as well, "I see you, 'What is the point of this exercise' thought. I see you 'Am I doing it right?' thought."

Now as you see those thoughts and feelings, wiggle your fingers and toes. "I see you thoughts and feelings, and I am moving my fingers and toes." Now continue to see your thoughts and feelings and lift your arms and give a gentle stretch. "I see you thoughts and feelings, and I am stretching." Acknowledge your thoughts and feelings and bring your attention to the room. What you can see and hear. Acknowledge the thoughts and feelings and breathe and open your eyes. "I see you thoughts and feelings, and I can move, hear, and see." Breathe.

Acceptance

In seeing and creating space for those experiences, you created a third response style: acceptance. Acceptance is being open to internal experiences without following or struggling with them. By letting go of the struggle, you can then choose where you want to put your energy. You can choose an action that moves you closer to what is important to you. One way of viewing acceptance is accepting the presence of something, whether or not you like it being there. When you accept the presence of something, other thoughts and feelings may emerge (such as sadness, anger, or fear). Upon accepting the presence of something you can then explore which way of responding would be consistent with your values and who you want to be. Acceptance can be a way of improving your efficiency, as you determine what is worth putting your energy towards. Sometimes the fight to get rid of or avoid discomfort is not worth it and moves you further away from who you want to be. Sometimes accepting the presence of discomfort creates space for you to move closer towards being the you that you want to be.

Acceptance is not:

- agreeing with it
- liking it
- giving in or giving up
- "sucking it up."

I grew up in Australia, and now live in Canada. One of the big differences between Australia and Canada is the weather. Every winter I have to deal with something that I did not grow up with—snow. I have struggled in different ways with snow (and my nemesis, ice). I have fantasized about being a snowbird, which is a term used for those who go somewhere warm during the winter months. If I was to become a snowbird I would see my loved ones in Canada less and it would impact my work, not to mention my bank account and the environment.

I have thrown myself into stomping around and complaining about snow and questioning why I moved here. The dumps of snow still happen, and as a result of throwing my energy into complaining I am more miserable, and not much fun to be around.

I have pretended that the snow isn't there, and thrown myself into doing things around the house, or curling up with a good book. Again, the snow still remains, and I am disconnected from seeing my loved ones and being active. It is not unusual that during my time of trying to avoid snow the weather conditions have changed, thus changing the snow from powdery fluffy stuff that is fun and easy to shovel, into a wet heavy mess or, worse still, ice. While I have enjoyed the brief break from snow, I have been disconnected from other things I enjoy, and the snow is now harder to deal with.

After many years of living here, I now accept snow and choose how I want to respond to it. I go out and shovel and look at it like a way of moving my body in service of my value of health. I put in my headphones and listen to a podcast or an audiobook in service of my value of knowledge. Once I have shovelled, I can get around and be connected to people and experiences important to me. The snow is still there, and I am living with it in a way that is more consistent with my values. Am I always happy to go out and shovel? No, but throwing my energy into how I don't like shovelling didn't achieve anything. Am I blocking or avoiding my thoughts and feelings? No, I'm acknowledging the frustration I feel as the plow pushes more snow into my driveway. I breathe and let the frustration be, as I continue shovelling.

Acceptance is often hard to achieve and maintain, thus you will still find me at times longing to be a snowbird, complaining or avoiding, even after many years of living in Canada.

Acceptance of the forest

Acceptance of the forest involves accepting that these uncomfortable thoughts and feelings are going to happen. They may get less intense or frequent at times, and other times they may be more intense and frequent. It sucks that they occur. It hurts. At times it may seem that life would be easier if they didn't occur, yet there those thoughts and feelings are.

Acceptance of the forest involves letting go of the fight to fix or avoid. When you notice urges to struggle, pause and compassionately acknowledge the presence of the uncomfortable thoughts and feelings, and identify what step would be consistent with the you that you want to be.

Acceptance involves accepting the discomfort that may come as you take those steps towards being the you that you want to be, as it is in service of something important to you. Acceptance and moving towards your values does not make all the discomfort go away. Often new forms of discomfort emerge, such as fear of the unknown. Acceptance is letting those feelings be there as they are part of the journey to you.

Choose your own adventure

Acceptance is new and it is a process; you may be very wary of it. That is okay. You can experiment and go on a choose your own adventure journey. You can take the path of fix it/problem-solve, avoid, or acceptance. Notice what happens when you take the different paths. Not in a judgmental way, but rather in a curious way.

You may be invited to an event with your friends. Your mind's response to the invite may be thoughts of, "I have gained so much weight, what will they say?" The discomfort may activate the fix it path, where you calculate how long till the event, and possible options to lose weight in that time. The discomfort may activate the avoidance path where you decide not to go to the event. Then there is the acceptance path, where you compassionately acknowledge the thoughts and feelings as they appear. You choose to go because connection with your friends is important to you. Observe and notice what happens in the short term and over time in each path.

A word of caution on your choose your own adventure journey: pace yourself. Some people want change so much and are so excited about trying something new that they launch themselves into the deep end of the acceptance pool and try to practice it in the most challenging of situations. For some, it is a sink or swim moment, and they manage to swim and build confidence from it. Many sink, are distressed, and vow never to jump in the pool again. Their mind lunges at them, "See I told you it wouldn't work. I don't know why you even tried."

Start in the shallow end. Some pools have markers on the side indicating the increasing depth of the pool. You can create your own version of these by writing down different situations, starting with the ones that would be least difficult to respond differently to (shallow end), and moving up to the most difficult (deep end). With curiosity and compassion, observe what happens when you respond with acceptance to a situation that you may usually respond to with avoidance or fixing/problem-solving.

MAPPING OUT YOUR POOL

Think of different situations, thoughts, or feelings that you could experiment with different responses (acceptance, fix it, or avoid), and place them in order of intensity. Starting in the shallow end (less intense feelings or less sticky thoughts), all the way up to the deep end (intense, overwhelming, or sticky thoughts). Notice what happens when you jump in at different places.

Shallow End: Situation with thoughts or feelings that are less intense or easier to sit with.

....

....

....

....

....

Deep End: Situation with thoughts or feelings that are very intense or hard to sit with.

Continuing in the forest

This is your forest. It is a part of you, and therefore may not disappear; struggling with it pulls you away from being you. You can't control whether the forest exists, but you can change the impact it has on you. You can see the trees. You can feel it pull or entangle you, and you can still take steps towards being the you that you want to be. Strategies discussed in the following chapters may help take the power off the thoughts and feelings that may emerge as you go further on your journey through the forest.

CHAPTER **SIX**

Take the Power Out of the Forest

It can sometimes feel like this forest is an enchanted forest with some wicked power that zaps you of your energy or puts you in a zombie-like trance, following the masses in pursuit of the ideal. But what if that power is an illusion, and we can take the power off the forest? Well, we can try through a skill called defusion. I must confess that I have been a bit sneaky and have been planting the seeds of defusion throughout this book. How I have phrased things and the use of the metaphor of the forest have been nudging you towards defusion. So, let us have a look at the enchanted forest and take the power out of the spell it has via defusion.

We think a lot

Our brain is programmed to think. Our ability to think and the way that we think have kept us alive. A recent study[65] extrapolated that on average people have over 6000 thoughts per day. Over six thousand thoughts. That is a lot of thoughts, and I'd say that there is a fair chance that not all of those 6000+ thoughts are accurate, important, or helpful (even among the smartest of people).

Are you able to control the content of all those 6000+ thoughts? Can you say to yourself, "I only want to think about cute fluffy kittens all day because that makes me smile?" Can you instruct your brain to have only positive thoughts and not distressing ones? Let's do a little experiment to see if you can control even some of those 6000+ thoughts. Think about a cute fluffy ginger kitten. Its fur is so soft, and its eyes are so wide and full of wonder. It is making those cute little kitten meowing sounds. Now set the stopwatch on your phone to a minute. Put the book down, and in that minute *do not* think about that cute fluffy ginger kitten. *Do not* bring the image to your mind. *Do not* say the words cute fluffy ginger kitten. Go ahead with your minute of *not* thinking about the cute fluffy ginger kitten.

How did you go? Were you able to not think about the kitten? Were you only able to not think about the kitten by consciously focusing your attention onto something else?

What experiments like these demonstrate is that we are not always able to control our thoughts. Thoughts are going to randomly pop into our head. Thoughts are going to appear in response to things happening around us: sights, sounds, and smells. We may not be able to choose which thoughts emerge. Given that we can't control what comes into our mind, where does that leave us? Well, we can look at how we respond when the thoughts come.

Some thoughts when we have them, we latch onto like they are absolute facts that are very important to us. We treat the thoughts as absolute truths or as being important. We hold onto them and play them over and over again. Those thoughts gain power, gather their friends, and are increasingly able to direct our behavior. But what if those thoughts are some of the many thoughts that may not be accurate, important, or helpful? That is a lot of power and energy going towards something that may not be accurate, important, or helpful.

If latching or holding onto thoughts give them more power and can lead to unhelpful actions, what other ways are there to respond to thoughts? What else can be done with them? How about we do a few more experiments, and curiously observe what happens?

THOUGHT EXPERIMENT 1: I'M HAVING A THOUGHT

The following exercise is very common in the ACT community since it was first conceived by a leader in the field, Dr. Steven Hayes, in 1999.

Bring a thought to mind that you sometimes get lost in (but not one that you get super stuck in). For example, "If I eat that I will get fat," or "I am fat." Play it in your head for a moment. Curiously observe your experience. Notice any thoughts that come with that thought. Notice any emotions that appear. Notice any sensations in your body.

Now add to the beginning of that, "I am having a thought that..." For example, "I am having a thought that if I eat that I will get fat," or "I am having a thought that I am fat." Play it in your head for a moment. Curiously observe your experience. Notice any thoughts that come with that thought. Notice any emotions that appear. Notice any sensations in your body.

Now add to the beginning of that, "I am noticing I am having a thought that..." For example, "I am noticing I am having a thought that if I eat that I will get fat," or "I am noticing I am having a thought that I am fat." Play it in your head for a moment. Curiously observe your experience. Notice any thoughts that come with that thought. Notice any emotions that appear. Notice any sensations in your body.

Many people notice that as they take each step a space is created between them and the thought, and the power of the thought is reduced. For some people, particularly with very strong/sticky thoughts, they may not notice a change. That is okay. If you observe this, maybe experiment with the same technique but with a different thought.

THOUGHT EXPERIMENT 2: FOREST VISUALIZATION

Throughout this book the metaphor of a forest has been used. In the previous sections we talked about how your forest came to be. This metaphor can be used to aid defusion from a thought. Take a moment and look at your forest.

If your body image thoughts were in the form of a tree, what would it be? Would it be a tree? Would it be a bush? Would it be a vine? Would it be prickly? Would it have thorns? How big is it? Would the different thoughts look different? Would the "I am fat" tree look the same as the "I am a failure tree?" Create the image in your mind or draw or paint or sculpt it out.

When you encounter the tree, how does it get you? Do you get stuck in the thorns or vines, or is it so imposing in its stature that you feel you can't move?

Visualize unhooking yourself from those thorns or vines or walking around or finding a hole in the imposing structure so you can keep going. Say to yourself, "Ah there is that tree again. There are a lot of them in this part of the forest."

Again, this exercise doesn't make the thoughts go away, but it helps you look at the thoughts in a different way.

THOUGHT EXPERIMENT 3: MY CONDITIONING

In the previous section we talked about how through your experiences you have been conditioned to have certain thoughts and feelings.

Bring to mind a body image thought. Run it through your mind for a moment. For example, "My thighs are too big." Curiously observe what emerges as you run this thought through your mind.

Now add to that, "My conditioning is telling me..." For example, "My conditioning is telling me my thighs are too big." Curiously observe what emerges as you run this thought through your mind.

Similar to what you did in the first exercise, let us take another step back: "I am noticing that my conditioning is telling me..." For example, "I am noticing that my conditioning is telling me my thighs are too big." Curiously observe what emerges as you run this thought through your mind.

THOUGHT EXPERIMENT 4: WORKABILITY

In the previous chapter we looked at struggle versus acceptance, and noticing the times when struggle moves you away from who you want to be.

Bring to mind a body image thought. For example, "I feel fat in this outfit." Ask yourself what happens when you stay with this thought, and it dictates what you do. Is that a helpful path? Does it move you closer to the you that you want to be?

Notice you are not asking if it is right or wrong, or true or false. You are asking if it is helpful to hand the power to this line of thinking?

Fusion versus defusion

Each of these experiments is a defusion exercise. The shift you may have experienced as you did the experiments is the movement from being fused to defused.

When you are fused with a thought you are treating it like it is an absolute truth, an order, something of utmost importance. When you are defused from a thought, the thought remains but the power is taken off it. The power of the enchanted forest is broken a little. The thought becomes just a thought that may or may not be true. With the power taken off the thought you are creating space to move, even with the presence of the thought. You are not changing the thought, but rather changing how you interact and relate with the thought.

While defusion can seem like a weird little exercise, there is a fair bit of theory and research that underlie it. Remember that web of associations of "good" and "bad" that we talked about in Chapter One? When you are doing defusion exercises you are adding threads to your web, and in adding threads a dilution happens, and other potential connections or threads can be made.

There are many defusion exercises, so if the ones in this book don't speak to you, there may be others out there that do speak to you. Different defusion techniques have been used on a variety of thoughts attached to different struggles (such as depression thoughts and anxiety thoughts), and it has been found that the intensity and impact of the thoughts decrease.

Troubleshooting defusion

These exercises sound simple, but as they are not how we usually interact with our thoughts, they can be more challenging than how they first appear.

- *"I couldn't do it."* Although there are similarities in how people's brains work, there are also differences. Some people's brains like and respond well to creating visual images, and can create a detailed image of their forest. Other people struggle to create visual images. Some people's brains respond more to words, and thus find it easier to access the "I'm having a thought" exercise.

There are many different defusion exercises, and some people create their own based on experiences that are meaningful to them. If one exercise didn't fit for you, keep experimenting with different defusion exercises and find one that fits your mind's strengths.

- *"It didn't work. I still think or feel_____."* The purpose of defusion is not to get rid of the thoughts or feelings, but rather to change how you interact with the thought and the power of it.
- *"What if the thought is true?"* In practicing defusion we are not stepping into a battle of truth, as that can be a form of struggling with the thought, and possibly of intensifying distress. Instead, we are looking at whether it is helpful, and whether it moves you closer to your values and who you want to be. If it is true but not helpful, we want to take the power off it. If it is true and helpful, you can let it be.
- *"What if it motivates me?"* A lot of thoughts can come from our inner critic. As much as it can be painful to hear from the inner critic, many people are fearful of not having it or taking power from it as they feel it motivates them and prevents things from getting worse. Often the inner critic's intent is self-improvement or protection. Unfortunately, for many people the words and the tone the inner critic uses have the opposite effect to the intent behind it. It can lead to reduced motivation and feelings of guilt and shame. This brings us back to the question of, is this thought helpful? Is this an effective way of motivating you? The fear of taking the power off the thought has provided you with information on an area that you may need help with within your journey: motivating yourself. Is there a kinder way to motivate yourself? Experiment with a compassionate nudge to yourself, like you would give a friend, and notice what happens.
- *"This is stupid. I don't see the point."* What happens when you stay with the thought of "This is stupid. I don't see the point," whether it is with this exercise or other things in life? I know when I get those thoughts, I become very stubborn and don't try whatever it is being suggested; the more that people try to convince me, the more I dig my heels in. There have been times I have not regretted that stance, and it hasn't impacted me at all. There have been other

> times where eventually I have tried what is being recommended and it has been helpful, or I enjoyed it. Then I would have thoughts of "I should have just done it when first asked." Other times I have done what was suggested, it wasn't helpful, and I then felt more comfortable and confident in my stance of "I hear you. I tried it, and these are the difficulties I encountered or why it didn't work for me." You don't lose anything from giving it a try.

Being someone who values adventure and openness, I have dabbled in circus arts. This includes aerial arts like silks and trapeze. Did I mention I am scared of heights?

Fearing heights, there have been many times that I had thoughts that would hook me. Thoughts that are not just words, but visualizations of things going horribly wrong. When I followed these thoughts and stayed with them, I would freeze. I could feel my body seize up and I couldn't move. I would decide that I couldn't do it and would bring myself off the apparatus. This would usually be followed by a barrage of self-critical thoughts, internal frustration, and disappointment with myself.

When I didn't follow the thoughts and images but defused from them instead, I was able to do the trick. It was exhilarating. I felt such a high. The thrill and sense of accomplishment are huge.

I was also the oldest and biggest of the class. This brought with it a series of body image thoughts, particularly when I saw pictures or videos and compared myself to my younger classmates. When fused with these thoughts, I didn't want to do aerial, and I didn't want pictures, videos, or to perform. Yet when I defused from the thoughts, I created space. What stepped into that space were thoughts of what I enjoyed about doing aerial and why I was doing it. In that space, I could move my attention to the present moment and focus on the strength and movement of my body. I owned that I was scared. I owned that I was different. I brought my character to the performance. Those around me could see that you can have the scary thoughts and feelings, and still do it. When I performed, I may not have been the stereotypical pretty or graceful aerial performer, but I'd like to think I entertained and inspired.

In the years of doing aerial, the thoughts never completely disappeared, but my strength in defusing them increased. Some days I was stronger than others. Some days I would be entangled in my thoughts. But over the years I was able to go higher and higher and perform more scary manoeuvers. I performed in front of loved ones on a trapeze with roller-skates on. I was my badass, adventurous, strong self.

What is the point of this story? It is okay to have the thoughts. It is okay to be scared. If I did defusion and took action purely with the intent of making the thoughts and feelings go away, I would have been disappointed and quit aerial within weeks. Defusion allowed me to take action. Action that in that moment was scary but was also so much fun and gave me a sense of achievement. I did that thing that I thought I couldn't.

CHAPTER **SEVEN**

My Emotions, My Signposts

Whether you navigate your body image trees via fixing/problem-solving, running/hiding, or acceptance, you will feel emotions. How do you feel about feeling? Do you identify with any of the following?

If I feel an emotion...

- I won't be able to get out of it
- I will get overwhelmed
- I will get stuck or immobilized
- I will do or say something I will regret
- I will waste time—there is no point in getting upset
- I won't know what to do
- It will be awful
- It won't matter
- I will have to do something different
- I will be weak/dramatic/attention-seeking
- I will lose control
- I will open the floodgates, and I don't know if I can close them
- Other: ....

How you view and respond to emotions has been shaped by your experiences and messages you received throughout your life about emotions, similarly to how you view and experience your body has been shaped by experiences and messages. These experiences may have involved people making direct statements like "Be strong, and don't cry," "Don't be so stupid," "Oh you are being over-dramatic. Can't you take a joke?" or "Oh don't worry about her. She is just wanting attention." The experiences may have involved nonverbal reactions when you were upset, such as rolling of the eyes, ignoring, or walking away. Alternatively, you may have watched the people around you never express many emotions, or only express them in extremes. What we can learn from these experiences is to doubt or fear how we feel, to shut the emotions down, and not show or express them to people around us.

Exploring messages you received about emotions

Take a moment to step back in your time machine. Set your time machine to "past" and "messages about emotions" and have a quick look at messages you received that have shaped how you respond to your emotions.

A guided version of this exercise can be found at www.jkp.com/catalogue/book/9781839977237.

MESSAGES ABOUT EMOTIONS

Time machine setting or when	What was happening?	What did you learn?	How did that impact your perception of and response to emotions?
Example: childhood	Example: I cried because someone made a hurtful joke and was told "Don't be so stupid. It was just a joke."	Example: It is not okay to cry, and the hurt I felt wasn't valid.	Example: To doubt my reactions, and to not cry in front of others.

SELF-REFLECTION QUESTIONS: MY EMOTION MESSAGES

- Throughout your life, how have people around you talked about and responded to emotions? Example: People didn't talk about emotions, and when a person cried, they were told they were being foolish and should be strong.
- What did you learn from those conversations and reactions? Example: Emotions are a sign of weakness, so don't show emotions.
- How did that impact your own ability to notice, respond to, and communicate your emotions? Example: I tend to block my emotions and when I do feel them, I don't show or communicate them with anyone.
- How has your response style to your own emotions impacted you? Example: On one hand it has kept me safe, but often I have felt very alone when I am going through a tough time.

Often through our experiences and learning, we come to view our emotions to be like big scary monsters. It makes sense that when we view them in this way, we fear them and do what we can to run from them. Yet often there is a cost to blocking emotions, and the emotions tend to remain and even get more intense.

What am I feeling?

Emotions are complex, and often we will experience multiple, at times seemingly conflicting, emotions at the same time. Given their complexity combined with what we may have learned about emotions, it makes sense that they can be hard to identify.

When you experience an emotion, your brain and body are noticing and responding to internal and external stimuli. The emotion is happening in a context. An example of an external context is you put on a pair of jeans that used to fit you and you find that they don't fit any more.

An example of an internal context is you experience a memory of a time when you were teased for your weight.

Your brain tries to make sense of or interpret this information. You may have the thought of "Oh no! I have gained weight. What will people think?" or "They didn't like me because of my weight." Over time and across contexts not only may the content of your thoughts change, but their movement may change as well. Your thoughts may race, or you may get stuck on one, or your mind may go blank. This is the thinking component of an emotion.

Your body also is responding. You may notice your body tensing up with fear, curling up in sadness, or your stomach churning with guilt, shame, or disgust. This is the physical component of emotions.

Your emotions alert and prepare you for action, so they usually have an action urge to them as well. You may notice urges to retreat and hide, or to look up options for diet and exercise. This is the action urge component of emotions.

You can then put a label on the emotion. Such as "This is anxiety" or "This is sadness."

The first step in identifying emotions is slowing down and checking in on the different components to see what you observe. Some people are really good at noticing the thinking part of their emotions, so when they start to notice and connect with emotions more, they start there. Other people notice the physical sensations the most, while yet others don't notice the thinking or the physical but instead notice the actions they take. Start in the component you believe is easiest for you. There may be some components you feel really disconnected from. That is okay. Learning to notice and identify your emotions is a skill that you can build and improve over time.

Let us take a moment now to check in on how you are feeling. A guided audio version of this exercise can be found at www.jkp.com/catalogue/book/9781839977237, and reflection questions to connect with your emotions can be found over the page.

GUIDED EXERCISE: NOTICING

First notice the "when" or the context, what has been happening today? Bring your attention to when you woke up, and what has occurred since then, bringing you up to this present moment. Just notice what happened. Don't judge. Just observe the events as they are.

Then move your attention to your body. Not to judge, but to notice sensations or physical presence of emotions. Start at your feet and scan your body, noticing any sensations, such as an unsettled feeling, or butterflies in the stomach, tension in the shoulders, tightness in the throat or jaw. Again, you are just observing. Not judging or trying to analyze.

Then move your attention to your thoughts, beginning with noticing the pattern of thinking. Are your thoughts racing? Do you feel like you're thinking through a fog? Do your thoughts keep moving back to one thing or area? What thoughts are taking up the most attention and space?

Now move your attention to any urges to take action. What action urges are you experiencing today? Are there urges to run, hide, or block? Or are there urges to fix, or problem-solve? What do the urges look and feel like?

If you feel able, try to label the feelings attached to what you noticed in your mind or body. Are you experiencing anxiety, sadness, or shame? What intensity are you experiencing that emotion? If you had to rate it on a scale of 1 to 10 (with 10 being most intense), what would you rate it? Are you experiencing multiple feelings at the moment?

As you check in on your emotions, just notice and observe. Notice if anything emerges as you observe the different components of the emotion(s). Notice urges to pull away. Notice any judgment thoughts. Keep bringing your attention back to noticing and describing your emotion(s).

SELF-REFLECTION QUESTIONS: A NOD TO EMOTIONS

With each of these questions, notice, observe, and describe. You don't need to analyze why. You don't need to judge. Just NOD: notice, observe, and describe.

- What has been happening today? For example, I was going to get up early to exercise, but I woke up feeling "blah" so hit snooze and slept in instead. I woke up over two hours later.
- What do you feel in your body? For example, overall, I feel stiff and achy. As I scanned my body, I noticed a feeling in my stomach and a heaviness around my shoulders.
- What thoughts are you having? For example, my thoughts are racing around how I haven't exercised today and have slept in. I have thoughts of: I have wasted the day. I should have exercised. I am so lazy. I can't do anything I set my mind to. No wonder I am fat.
- Are you having any action urges? If so, what urges are you experiencing? For example, give up and go back to bed.
- Are you able to identify or label your emotions? If so, what are you feeling? For example, guilt, shame, sadness, and fear.
- Did any other thoughts, feelings, or action urges emerge as you turned towards your emotions? If so, what? For example, I thought the exercise was stupid and it would just make me wallow even more in how I am feeling, but as I did it, it felt like I was outside watching it. Like the emotions weren't pushing me around as much.

I feel because I care

In my office I often hear people say that they just want the feelings to go away. They don't want to feel. The only way I could ever take away a person's ability to feel would be if I could take away a person's ability to care about things, and all the brain machinery involved in this. I wouldn't want to do that, as it would take away so much of a person's experience of life.

If we didn't care about things, whether it is at an evolutionary or instinctual level, or at a value-based level, we wouldn't feel. Our brains are programmed to feel emotions. Let us take a moment to look at some common emotions (fear, sadness, guilt, shame, anger, happiness, and love), and what they tell us about what we care about.

Fear

Fear at the most instinctual level alerts us to danger or threats to survival. At a broader level, we experience fear when there is a threat to something important to us. As many of us have experienced fear in relation to our body or weight, it can be easy to assume that we care about our weight and body. But let us dig a little deeper, if the world didn't care about body weight and shape, if all the experiences of weight discrimination and stigma were no longer present, would you still have a fear reaction to weight?

Often the fear we experience is not about weight or body itself, but what we have learned to attach to it. Taking a moment to ask yourself "What is attached to weight?" allows you to look closer at what is important to you that is being threatened (real or perceived), and therefore activating the fear response. From there, you can explore more direct ways of getting needs met and connecting with what is important to you. More on that in later chapters.

Fear tells us that something important to us is being threatened.

Sadness

Sadness tends to occur when we lose or are disconnected from something that is important to us. We may experience sadness when we look in the mirror or get on the scale. We may assume that we are sad about our body, but again it is not the body itself that creates the sadness, it is how society responds to the body and what we have learned to associate with the body. For example, if you associate loneliness with a certain body size, and then see yourself as being that size, you will likely have thoughts that you are (or will be) lonely. This may lead to feelings of sadness if being connected to others is important to you. When experiencing sadness, ask what is it that is important to me that I have lost or feel disconnected from right now?

Sadness tells us we are disconnected from or lost something that is important to us.

Guilt and shame

We often lump guilt and shame together, but there is a difference between the two emotions. Guilt is an emotion experienced when you did (or perceived that you did) something wrong. Shame is experienced when you perceive your whole self or who you are as being wrong or bad. Our mind often combines the two with thoughts of "If I do bad, then I am bad."

Both guilt and shame provide us with information on what is important to us, as they emerge when actions or self-perceptions are at odds with our values, how we want to behave and who we want to be. To separate guilt and shame, identify the behavior that you don't like, and then explore how it conflicts with the person you want to be. For example, you may lie to get out of an event because of how you feel about your body. You feel guilty because you don't like the behavior of lying. You may feel shame because you view yourself as an honest person, and this behavior conflicts with that.

Guilt and shame tell us that the actions that we are taking or how we perceive ourselves are not congruent with actions we want to take and the identity we want to hold.

Anger

Anger is often viewed in a negative way and is associated with harmful or negative actions (such as violence). Yet anger in and of itself is not a bad emotion. It alerts us to threats, injustices, or boundary violations. It can provide energy to allow us to take action against a threat. Anger is like fear in that it alerts us to a potential threat to what is important to us.

We tend to like to feel in control and that we have a sense of agency. When we notice that we are unable to do things we think we should be able to do (such as lose weight), we may experience self-directed anger. This is because not being able to do something we think we should be able to do threatens our sense of control and agency, not to mention the perceived danger that we may associate with the outcomes of not having control. When we see weight discrimination, we get angry. We get angry because we care about fairness, kindness, and the welfare of others. Weight discrimination runs smack against this.

Anger tells us that something we care about is being threatened in some way.

Love and happiness

We experience love and/or happiness when we are connected to or moving towards what is important to us. When you think of a time that you were happy, what were you connected to that is important to you? Some people state that they were happy when they lost weight or were at a lower weight. Again, let us dig a little deeper; what were you connected to or closer to when you lost weight or were at a lower weight? Was it a sense of achievement? Was it a connection with others? Was it being able to do or experience different things? The more connected you can be to what is important to you, the more likely you will experience love or happiness.

However, pain and pleasure are opposite sides of the same coin. What brings you love or happiness when you move towards it can bring other emotions like fear, anger, sadness, or guilt when you move away. Some people when they experience love or happiness also experience fear, as they fear that the connection they have will become threatened. People with a history of trauma, or who have had limited experience of love or happiness, will be more prone to this.

Love and happiness tell us that we are connected to or close to something that is important to us.

SELF-REFLECTION: WHAT ARE MY EMOTIONS TELLING ME?

Take a moment to see what your emotions are telling you about what is important to you.

Fear

- When do I tend to experience fear? For example, I feel fear when having to attend a wedding or another event where I have to dress up.
- What am I fearful will occur? For example, I fear that people will notice how I look, and think I am lazy or stupid. I fear that they won't like me or that I will be rejected.
- What is it that I care about that is being threatened? For example,

connection with others and belonging, and personal perception of achievement.

Sadness

- When are times that I have experienced sadness? For example, I feel sad when I see people post about something that I declined to go to.
- What is happening to what I care about (such as, has there been a loss or a disconnection)? For example, I am disconnected from my loved ones and activities that I enjoy.

Guilt and shame

- When have I experienced guilt and/or shame? For example, when I have not stood up for someone when a weight comment has occurred.
- How were my behaviors or how I view myself in conflict with how I want to behave and be seen? For example, I value acceptance and kindness, and the inaction behavior enabled the other person's judgmental and unkind behavior to continue.

Anger

- When do I tend to experience anger? For example, I experience anger when I or someone else is treated differently because we look different.
- What is it that I care about that is being threatened? For example, my values of kindness and justice are being threatened, as are connection and belonging.

Happiness and love

- When do I tend to experience happiness and/or love? For example, I feel happiness when I am traveling the world, experiencing new things, and connecting with people.
- What is present that I care about or feel connected to? For example, I am more present and connected to values of adventure, openness, and learning, as well as connected to people.

Take action to connect with what is important

In life we are going to care about things. We are going to care about multiple things. That is a good thing. It gives life meaning and vibrancy, but the cost of that is we will feel uncomfortable emotions. It is not possible to get through life without the things we care about being threatened in some way, shape, or form. Often in order to protect one thing you care about, another may take a hit. You may experience a values conflict.

While using our emotions to help gather information about what is important to us can be helpful to direct our actions, it does not make the uncomfortable emotions go away. Often, we are left asking what do I need in the face of this uncomfortable emotion? What will help me keep going in the face of this emotion?

Let's look at this in relation to the example of feeling fear when going to an event where you may experience people making appearance-related judgments and actions. The fear may be alerting you to a sense that connection and belonging is being threatened. Choosing to not go to the event would remove the discomfort of fear as you wouldn't be facing the threat to connection and belonging of appearance-related judgments and actions. Yet it would likely lead to guilt and sadness, as you would be stepping away from the potential of connection and belonging. No matter which action you take, you will experience some form of emotional discomfort.

Yet your emotions are providing you information on what is important to you, which opens the door to asking the question, "What can I do to connect with what is important to me?" You will feel some discomfort either way, but discomfort felt in the service of something important to you will likely be more bearable. In this example, going to the event and connecting with people you love would likely bring some anxiety, and it is in service of connection and belonging. Which brings me to the next important question, "What do I need to do to help me keep going when I feel this emotion?" The words that came to mind were breathing, soothing, and compassion.

Tools to keep moving in the face of the emotion

Breathe

I remember having a knee injury when I was young and calling my mum to tell her about it. She could hear I was upset, and her response was, "Just breathe." Teenage me was not impressed with this response, felt very invalidated, and went on a rant about how dare she tell me to "just breathe" when my life was ruined. I can sometimes see a flicker of this kind of response in the eyes of my clients when I talk about breathing exercises. I get it. I do.

Yet, there is a reason why breathing is encouraged. First, we do need to breathe. It is important to our survival. Second, breathing helps us override that fight/flight danger alert system. If our lives were in peril at that moment, we wouldn't have time to settle our breathing. Being able to settle the breath helps send a message to the brain, in a language it understands in that moment, that we are safe and not in immediate danger. Also, while we are focusing on our breath, our attention is likely away from the thoughts that may be ramping our emotions up.

Box breath

A very common breathing exercise is called box breathing. In this exercise you breathe in, to a count of 3. You can draw with your finger or imagine drawing a horizontal line as you breathe in. Then you hold your breath for 3 seconds, drawing a line down as you do this. Then release your breath to the count of 3, drawing another horizontal line. Finally holding again to the count of 3 and drawing a vertical line to complete the box. Repeat 3–7 times.

This exercise slows your breath, and in focusing on the counting and/or the box, attention is pulled away from thoughts that may be increasing distress.

Slow the breath

Many people, particularly when they are feeling anxious, are unable to get their breath into the flow of box breathing. Trying to can make them get more anxious, as they worry that they aren't doing it right or that their breathing is seriously wrong, and they can't control it. If this sounds familiar, let go of trying to fit your breath into a set rhythm. Instead, with each breath you take try to make it a little deeper, and a little slower. Slow your breath by slowing the rate of inhale and exhale. It may take a number of breaths for you to feel like you are getting a deep breath.

Some people find it helpful to count how many breaths they took in one minute, and then try to reduce that number.

Soothe

What do you do when a child or infant is upset, and you can't talk them down? You soothe them. You speak to them in a low calming or soothing voice. You give them a hug or swaddle them in a blanket. Through the senses, you send the message that they are safe and okay. That part of our brain that is soothed by senses doesn't disappear as we get older. It is still there, and during times of distress we can use it to take the edge off the distress.

Take a moment and think of your five senses (see, hear, touch, taste, and smell), and see if you can identify something that is soothing for each of them. Ideally, what you identify is something that can be portable, so you can take it with you when you are engaging in things that might be uncomfortable but move you closer to what is important to you.

SELF-REFLECTION EXERCISE: SOOTHING SENSES

- What visual stimuli do you find soothing? For example, connect with natural scenery (trees, ocean, sunset, mountains) via looking out the window or having pictures on your phone; sight of a loved one via looking towards them or picture you have; soothing colours.
- What auditory stimuli do you find soothing? For example, music, peaceful sounds, sound of a loved one's voice, absence of sound.
- What tactile sensations do you find soothing? For example, petting an animal, texture of clothing or blanket, jewelery, fidget toys.
- What tastes do you find soothing? For example, warm beverages (tea, coffee, hot chocolate), candy, mints.
- What scents do you find soothing? For example, favorite moisturizer or soap, ocean, fresh cut grass.

Compassion

Have you ever had a friend or a loved one who's going through a really tough time come to you with their distress, and there is not a thing you can do to fix it or make it go away? What do you do? You are there for them. You are there with them in their distress. You show them compassion.

You can be a compassionate presence for yourself. You can kindly acknowledge the emotion, the struggle, how hard it is, and that it makes sense that it is there. Whether or not you are able to take a step towards connecting with what is important to you, you can still extend kindness to yourself. You can be a friend or a mate to yourself.

Take a moment and think about what you would say to a friend to help them keep going, even though things are tough. Imagine saying that to yourself.

Some people find self-compassion really challenging. While they are practicing becoming more skillful with it, they turn to a compassionate other person. They may bring their partner or a friend to the event, because their loved one understands that they will be anxious and will be there with them in that anxiety because they know it is important to them.

My own signposts?

If you have done the exercises in this chapter, you may be building an awareness of what your emotions look like, what they are telling you about what is important to you, and what you may need to help you keep moving towards what is important to you in the face of your emotions. That is a lot of information, so let us pull it all together and turn it into a signpost. Instead of your emotions being like a monster that you frantically try to fight or get away from, they become signposts drawing your attention to information that may be helpful for you to proceed.

WIIFI

When I step out of my comfort zone, like most people, I experience fear. When I turn towards my fear, I notice a theme of "What if I f**k it up?" The "f**k it up" could be something related to weight or appearance, or it could be my own actions. It is a fear of something happening to threaten my connection with others or the work that I do to help others.

My go-to response in the past was to avoid, and not put myself out there. If I don't put myself out there, I can't mess it up. Continue hiding away from the spotlight.

By slowing down, noticing my emotions, and paying attention to what they were telling me about my feelings, I could see how my actions were moving me away from what was important to me, and thus why I would feel guilt or sadness. What I was needing when I felt fear was to connect with people and my work, not run from them. I needed comfort, compassion, and soothing in the face of the anxiety to help me take action while the anxiety was present. The comfort, soothing, and compassion wouldn't necessarily prevent me from failing, but they help me be kind to myself and feel that I would be okay even if things don't go as planned.

Yet to remember all that, particularly in the heat of the moment, can be challenging, so I have created a signpost for myself: "WIIFI." Just like when I am traveling and see a "Wi-Fi" sign I get connected; when I see my own internal "WIIFI" sign it alerts me that I am feeling anxious, something important to me is in danger, and that I need to take steps to get connected. Sometimes when traveling and connecting to "Wi-Fi" I can connect right away, and sometimes I need to take a few extra steps (like figure out what to connect to and the password) to get connected. When I see "WIIFI" sometimes I can connect right away, and other times I need to take steps of breathing, soothing, or compassion to help me connect or stay connected. Turning my anxiety into this image helps take the power out of it and allows me to take steps towards what is important to me.

Create your signpost

Take a moment now, think of your emotions, what they tell you about what is important to you, and what you need when they emerge. Are you able to turn that information into a signpost? It may be one that is like an information panel, or it may be an image like a caution sign. You may want to create multiple signs for different emotions. You may not want to create a sign at all and carry forward information gained without turning it into a signpost. Do whatever suits how your brain works.

Summary

Throughout life you will encounter emotions because we are programmed to experience emotions; we experience them because we care. Although our emotions can be very uncomfortable, and we may want to block them, they have helped humans survive and thrive for many years. Emotions provide us with a wealth of information, and if we turn towards our emotions, we can gather the information and use it to connect with what is important to us. When things are going smoothly this can be easier, but often things don't go smoothly. During these times our emotions can be particularly intense, and we need help so we can keep moving and take action consistent with our values. Breathing, soothing, and compassion can be used to help you take action even when the emotions are present in an intense manner. You don't need to run and hide when an emotion appears in your forest (like you would from a scary monster); you can turn towards and shine your light towards it to see and read the signpost that is your emotion.

CHAPTER **EIGHT**

Change the Story

Throughout our lives we are constantly exposed to stories. We read them. We watch them. Those around us tell them. We tell them. Stories help us make sense of the world, those within it, and how they all interact. We learn through stories. In each of the stories we hear or tell, there are characters. When a character is made and labeled there are often expectations of how they should and should not behave, and how others should and should not react to them.

Imagine watching the following characters in a movie or a show; are there behaviors that you would expect from them? Are there any behaviors that would surprise you if they came from them? How do you think others would respond to them?

- The thin one.
- The fat one.
- The mean one.
- The smart one.
- The failure.
- The friendly one.

What you may have noticed is that there are assumptions and rules attached to each of the characters that impact what we expect to see in their behaviors or story. Over the course of our lives, we have learned these assumptions and rules from our experiences. We often aren't consciously aware of them.

My character: My story

We all have stories that we tell ourselves. Us and those around us are characters in those stories. We may not realize we are doing it, nor may we realize the impact of these stories, but these stories do have an impact.

If your character "always fails" or "is never good enough," and you look at your life, chances are your attention will move to all the times in your life where you failed or weren't good enough. When you look to the future, what you see and the actions you take may be limited as you have thoughts of "What is the point? I am just going to fail anyway."

How you view your body is part of your character. In being "the fat one" your mind may move towards the weight stigma noted earlier in the book. When you look to the future, fear may come up, along with thoughts of, "The fat one can't do that," or "They will laugh at the fat one."

If you have always been the character of "the thin one" and you start to gain weight you are likely to become distressed, because how you see yourself and how others may see you is being threatened and changed.

SELF-REFLECTION MOMENT: MY CHARACTERS

- What characters have you played or do you currently play in your life? For example, "the fat one," "the athletic one," "the failure," "the one who always..."
- What thoughts, feelings, and behaviors are connected to each of these characters? Including thoughts about what you can or can't do, actions taken based on this, feelings of anxiety or shame.
- How has being this character impacted you over time? For example, I stopped trying new things or putting myself out there because I thought I would fail, or people would judge me.

Typecast

Have you ever seen someone who acts become typecast? When an actor/actress becomes typecast, we make assumptions about the characters they will play, and what they will do. If someone is typecast in a more comedic role, when they try to move to a more dramatic role, we struggle to take them seriously, and may be waiting for them to crack a joke. Those in the industry often do what they can to prevent or fight against typecasting as it narrows the roles they can try for and play.

We can typecast ourselves. We can get locked into a particular character, and all the assumptions, rules, thoughts, feelings, and actions that come with it follow us around. We, and those around us, expect us to behave in a certain way because we have been typecast. Just like an actor/actress's potential roles narrow as a result of typecasting, our lives can also narrow.

SELF-REFLECTION MOMENT: HAVE I TYPECAST MYSELF?

- Have there been times in your life when you have been typecast?
- Which character(s) got typecast?
- How did it impact you (your thoughts, feelings, actions)?
- Are you stuck in a typecast now?

Breaking the typecast: Change the story

When we are typecast in a character our world shrinks. Yet we, as people, are really complex. We are not just one character on a narrow story arc. Who we are is a rich tapestry of multiple characters in different environments, interacting with other characters, woven together over time.

What is really cool is that we are the authors of our character and our stories. There is a part of us that can notice the different characters and storylines, and move our attention and energy in different directions, adding complexity to the characters and changing the story.

Let us do a quick thought experiment. Imagine "the fat one" going to a party. How might they behave, or interact with other people? Now imagine "the fat, kind one." How might they behave or interact with other people? Finally, what about the "fat, kind, fiery, badass?" How might they behave or interact with other people? Did you notice any changes in the story as more was added?

What many people notice is the more that is added to the character, the more potential actions and responses start to appear. In being the author of your own character and story, you don't need to erase (often nor can you) aspects of who you are. Yet that doesn't mean you are condemned to follow a narrow story, like the narrow story society attaches to weight. You can add aspects of who you are, or who you want to be, and in doing so you create options for yourself and others. Your character and story doesn't have to be all about weight or appearance, it can go far beyond that. You don't have to let society or others write your story.

Troubleshooting some common traps

- *"I have to be perfect."* I don't know about you, but when reading books or watching movies or shows, I have more of an appreciation of complex characters that have strengths and flaws. There is a vulnerability in those that have flaws that make them accessible and relatable, while I struggle to connect with the ones that are "perfect" or "flawless." In the vulnerability there is humanity, and the point of connection. Your character doesn't have to be "perfect" or "flawless." While your strengths are part of what makes you, so are your flaws. They are endearing. They can bring comic relief. They can be ways of connecting with others. They don't need to be parts of your character that you hide from others in a cave of shame.
- *"I have to be consistent or the same, all the time."* Different people know different parts of me. What people will see may vary depending on the context in which they see me. When working as a therapist when someone is being vulnerable, the kind, compassionate part of me steps forwards. Back when I was playing roller derby it wasn't the kind, compassionate me on the track; it was the fiery badass. Many people talk about this kind of experience with me in the therapy room. They have thoughts of "Am I being fake?" or "What is the real me?" Different environments, including the

people you are around, will draw out the different parts of you. That is normal. It is all still you.

- *"I don't know who I am," and "What if I make the wrong choice?"* Many of the people I work with express that they have been so disconnected from who they are and what is important to them, that they aren't sure what is true to them. They may express fear of choosing or creating the "wrong" character or story. Yet it is normal for things to change over time; aspects of our self or character that we may have been connected to years ago may not remain in the present-day context. The world around us changes. We change. It is normal; it is okay. If you give something a try and it doesn't feel like you, you are not stuck with it. You can try on different characters. In trying on different characters and being connected to your emotions you can learn what feels true to you.
- *"I have to follow the rules."* In our lives we are exposed to a lot of information. To help make sense of it all and determine what next steps to take, we create rules. If you hear words like "should," "shouldn't," "have to," or "must," there is probably a rule at play. Rules at times can be helpful, but at other times they keep us unnecessarily confined to a box. There are lots of rules around weight, such as rules around what people of different sizes should or should not be wearing or eating. Many of the societal rules around weight are not accurate or helpful. If a rule isn't accurate or helpful for you, then break or bend it. This is your story; you create the rules.
- *Thinking the character versus doing the character.* I have had other people try to tell my character and my story, and it has been very different to who I am. I have been frustrated that they saw me in that way, and that those to whom they told the story bought into the character and story without questioning or fact-checking with me. Yet, when I stepped back and looked at how much of my character I had shown people, it was very little. Of course, other people then filled in the blanks. Of course, the filled-in blanks weren't questioned, as others weren't able to see the inconsistency that I knew existed. If you add to your character, demonstrate it in your actions, otherwise people won't know it is there and they will

fill in the blanks themselves. You may not like what they fill it with, especially if it is based on weight stigma. If you add kindness to your character, do things that convey to others that you are kind. These don't have to be big things (like giving elaborate gifts). It could be as simple as facial expressions, asking someone how their day has been, or being polite.

ADD TO YOUR CHARACTER: WRITE YOUR STORY

It is now time to start exploring the complex character that is you and explore possible future chapters that could be written in your story.

1. Take a moment, think of, and write down your character as it has been (the narrower version).
2. Write a brief story arc for them capturing a little of the past, the present, and then moving into the future.
3. Return to your original character description. Think about what is important to you, who you want to be, and other elements of who you are, and use that to guide what you add to your character description.
4. Rewrite the next chapters of the story based on the character updates. Write about what they do differently that shows the world that this is who they are in all their complexity (strengths and flaws). Write how they break or bend rules to be true to themselves.
5. Remember that the story is not set in stone. Life is complex and always changing. As are we. Hold your story lightly.
6. Notice any thoughts or feelings that come up as you write. If they strongly pull you away, draw on some of the things discussed in previous chapters to help you experience them without being consumed by them.

The story of you in the forest

Earlier in the book I wrote about the different ways people navigate the body image trees. The story of bending to fit but never being enough, and the story of hiding in the shadows to stay safe. These don't have to be the only stories of navigating the forest. In adding to your character, you could be planting and nurturing other forms of trees. Or you could be adding to how you move through the forest; maybe blasting some music and dancing your way around. You are the author, what do you want to do in your forest?

CHAPTER **NINE**

Correcting the Misguided Route to Belonging

When I was first writing this book, this chapter didn't exist. It wasn't in the outline. However, belonging seems to be at the heart of many of our actions. We have this inbuilt yearning to belong, yet the ways we have learned to pursue belonging are far from effective. With technology and the internet, we have more ways than ever to connect with each other, yet at the same time we are increasingly feeling alone and our needs to belong are not being met.

Fitting in versus belonging

For many people, the pursuit of looking a certain way (including weight loss) is a pursuit of connection and belonging. The hiding and holding back, often seen and experienced in people with body image struggles and internalized weight stigma, often come from a sense of not being able to connect or belong because one is not meeting an appearance-based prerequisite for belonging.

These struggles are born out of an assumption that "in order to belong, I need to change to fit the group." Naturally, from this assumption we look to the world around us to try to determine who belongs, and what we need to do to be part of the group. In the appearance-focused world we live in, we are surrounded by images and people commenting on weight and body, and quickly learn that how we look is important to belonging. The fitness, cosmetic, diet, and beauty industries are all there lining up to take our money to "help" us meet the appearance or weight prerequisite so we can belong in society. Yet for many, achieving the ideal isn't possible, and even if it was it still wouldn't be enough to give that true sense of belonging. It would merely give a sense of fitting in.[66]

While the actions make sense given the assumption they are based on, they don't lead to the results we are seeking because the assumption itself is not accurate or helpful. Belonging involves being seen and accepted for who you are by another or by a group. It has a feeling component of a sense of security, safety, familiarity, and connection. If you have to change yourself to belong, you are not being seen or accepted for who you are, and thus you are fitting in (not belonging). The changing to fit in may provide a brief feeling of comfort or safety, but it is followed by a fear of "what if they see the real me?" Not to mention the inner sense of sadness and betrayal that comes when you turn your back on a part of you that makes you who you are.

SELF-REFLECTION MOMENT: FIT IN OR BELONG

- Does this sound familiar? Are there times that you fitted in, but didn't feel like you belonged?
- What are things that you have done to try and fit in, or in the pursuit of belonging?
- What parts of you did you shun or turn your back on?
- What happened? What was the connection like? How did you feel?

Belonging from the inside

If the assumption "in order to belong, I need to change to fit the group" isn't accurate or helpful, where does that leave us?

Often when we think about belonging, we get focused on connection with other people, which is important, but, as we see with fitting in, connection alone does not bring a sense of belonging. If the quality of connection is poor, or what the person is connecting with isn't really us, then we won't feel a sense of belonging. Let us move our focus to the other part of belonging; to be seen and accepted for who we are. There are two components to this. The first is knowing and being true to who we are, and the second is allowing ourselves to be seen.

Who am I?

Throughout our lives we can get pulled in many different directions and get caught up in just going through the motions. Existing, but not living. Connecting, but not meaningfully. The fast pace of life can mean we don't give ourselves the time to slow down and ask, what do I really want to stand for? In Part Two of this book, you slowed down, reflected, and looked at your values. This was a step towards knowing and being true to yourself. We are now going to connect with this further by imagining a world where many of the things that have held you back from being yourself are not as present.

Imagine that we have tinkered with the time machine that we previously used and have created another setting. In this new setting you can travel to an alternate world. In this world, there is less focus on weight and appearance. In this world, you didn't grow up surrounded by appearance- and weight-related judgment. In this world there is increased acceptance of people regardless of how much they weigh or how they look. When people talk and connect with each other, they do so through shared interests and ideas, not through appearance and judgment. Imagine waking up in this world and going about your day. Would you start your day differently? Would you wear different clothes? Would the rest of your day unfold differently? If you didn't have to worry about how you looked and what you weighed, what would you want to put your energy into? How would you interact with the people around you? Continue to imagine this world and connect with the you within it. This is you being you. This is you being more than your body and your weight.

For a guided audio version of this go to www.jkp.com/catalogue/book/9781839977237.

As with many of the exercises within this book, you may want to write down what you noticed.

SELF-REFLECTION MOMENT: DIFFERENT WORLD

- What thoughts emerged as you stepped into and traversed this alternate world?
- What feelings did you experience when you first entered the world, and as you continued to explore and connect with yourself?
- What actions did you imagine doing in this alternate world? Were they the same or different to what you do now?
- Did you interact with people differently in this alternate world? How were you different? How were other people's responses different?
- What did the exercise help you notice in relation to who you want to be and being true to yourself?

In this, and many of the exercises throughout this book, you have connected with who you are. The memories and parts of you that you are proud of, and the memories and parts that you are less proud of. They are all what makes you, you. A complex human who is strong, yet vulnerable. You are enough as you are. You don't need to fix and contort to build a sense of belonging. Brené Brown aptly put it in *Braving the Wilderness*, "True belonging doesn't require that we change who we are; it requires that we be who we are."[67]

Being seen

Knowing who you are gives something for others to connect with and is thus a step closer to feeling a sense of belonging with others. The next step involves being open to letting that self be seen, but we often get in our own way. We want to be seen, but at the same time are so scared of being seen. We want to be seen and we also have thoughts that if we are seen as we are, people will see our flaws and will judge or criticize or reject. Our brain then moves into problem-solving mode, exploring how we can minimize the flaws, and thus minimize the risk of being criticized. We may throw ourselves into trying to be perfect, pleasing people, or carefully curating what we let others see.

I remember from a very young age I felt uncomfortable being seen. I didn't like when people would watch me play, even if it was just my parents or siblings checking to see if I was okay. I also recall moments as a child when I had been laughed at when being me, being playful, being excited, or being scared. In hindsight, the laughter in those moments was sometimes coming from a place of love (we often laugh when children say or do things so innocent and cute) or playful jest. Yet back then, when I heard the laughter, I thought I was doing something wrong, which made me want to hide. Two stories became present in my mind that impacted my openness to being seen, one in relation to myself and one in relation to others. The story I had about myself was that I wasn't good enough to be seen. The story I had in relation to those around me was that they would judge and hurt me. In response to these stories, I would oscillate between hiding, and being the good girl. I would strive to achieve, and if I wasn't good, it was only a matter of time before I would quit because not being good at something felt scary and threatening to me. The thought of, "People will like you if you are good" drove my actions. Academia was the path where this manifested the most, and I worked hard to be good enough to be seen. I did get praise for my grades, and my striving did help me on my career path, and it also brought distress along the way. I was only open to being seen when I felt I was "good enough," and outside of that I would find different ways to hide as I wasn't good enough and the world was not a nice place.

Take a moment to read the following sentences and notice how your mind completes each one:

I can't be seen until...

In order to be seen I must...

If people saw the real me...

How you complete these sentences can point towards some thoughts or self stories that get in the way of being seen. One cluster of thoughts or self stories that reduce openness to being seen are those which we have about ourselves. These thoughts can look like a list of prerequisites that have to be met in order to feel safe or worthy of being seen. The thoughts could be a general statement of "good enough" or "not good enough." The thoughts could also be a set of rules about what you can or can't do based on your body. For example, "I can't start dating until I lose weight," or "In order to be seen I must look perfect—hair, make-up, clothes must be on point."

How we view others and the world around us can also impact whether or not we allow ourselves to be seen. If we perceive others as mean, judgmental, or dangerous, of course we wouldn't open ourselves to the vulnerability of being seen. If there is a history of trauma or being hurt in the past, these thoughts may emerge as a means of trying to protect us from being hurt again. These externally focused thoughts that impede being seen can look like an interpersonal version of "I can't..., until..." such as, "I can't be open, until I know they are trustworthy." The thoughts could also take the form of assuming what people are thinking or how they would respond. For example, "I can't post that pic on social media because then that person will say how much weight I have gained, and another will think I am lazy. So, I just won't post anything."

When we hold onto these thoughts and stories tightly, it impacts our actions. If we see ourselves as deeply flawed and unworthy of connection and belonging, and the world around us as judgmental and unsafe, it makes sense that we either won't put ourselves out into the world, or we put ourselves out into the world in a way that we fit in (as opposed to our authentic self). These are protective responses that would likely reduce fear and distress in the short term but would likely create distress and move people further away from connection and belonging.

SELF-REFLECTION MOMENT: WHAT PREVENTS ME FROM BEING SEEN?

- Have your thoughts or self stories about your body impacted your openness to being seen?
- Are there any thoughts or stories about other people that have impacted your openness to being seen?
- What do you do when these thoughts and stories show up? What actions do you take to not be seen?
- How have these actions helped you?
- How have these actions hindered you?

Being seen involves being vulnerable. An act of vulnerability that could lead to a forming and strengthening of an authentic connection and a sense of belonging can also open ourselves up for judgment, attack, or rejection. It makes sense that we can fear being seen, but that fear does not have to completely dictate our actions and push us into hiding.

Being seen is not an all or nothing phenomenon. We don't have to show all of us, to all people, all the time. You can determine with whom and where you want to show up in an authentic manner. Using the tools you have already found in this book, you can lightly hold onto the thoughts and stories that have impeded being seen, and create space for different ways of showing up. When you feel that pull to hide, you may take a moment to say to yourself, "I am noticing I am having thoughts and urges to hide." You may even draw on some self-compassion, acknowledging that it makes sense to have urges to hide when you feel vulnerable. You may notice whether that fear is telling you something about what is important to you. Maybe you are experiencing fear because authentic connection is important to you, and you don't want to jeopardize that. If authentic connection is important to you, then think about what you need to help facilitate that and see if you can turn towards your values to help guide your actions.

Small steps to being seen and creating connection

Look up

Often when people think of being seen or connecting with others, their mind jumps ahead to bigger steps, such as sharing personal stories and forming close friendships. While that may be nice, it can also put a lot of pressure on actions and interactions. This can create heightened distress and send us quickly back into hiding or people-pleasing. It can be more helpful to take small steps towards connection and being seen. One such small step is to make eye contact with people. Notice the color of their eyes. Maybe, if it fits, give them a soft, warm, authentic smile. You can do this with people with whom you already have a connection, and with people you see day-to-day. Notice what you experience and notice how others respond.

There is a park near where I live, where I regularly go for walks or runs. When I first started going there, I was in hiding mode. I would look down and not make eye contact with those I passed. I started to experiment with making eye contact with people. I noticed that upon making eye contact with people, they would often smile and give a nod or say hello. When that happened, I could feel a softening or lightening within me. I then started also smiling, giving a nod of acknowledgment, and saying hello. I noticed that on the walks or runs where most of the interactions with people went this way, I felt better than on the ones where I had my head down or when those interactions didn't happen as much. Just that simple act of looking up, kindly acknowledging another person, and having them reciprocate, created such a shift.

Find your voice

For many of us, not being seen has involved either not speaking, or using our voice to speak other people's words (such as, saying what we thought others wanted us to say). Having an authentic voice is part of the journey of being seen. Having an authentic voice involves vocalizing your needs, wants, ideas, and feelings. When you have a voice, you are present in the conversation. Having a voice doesn't have to be the sharing of your deepest desires. Having a voice could be stating a preference in selection of food or a movie. I don't know about you, but there have been times in my life when I have robbed myself of my own voice. When someone asked, "What do you want?" I would say things like, "Whatever everyone else is having," or "It's okay. You can choose." In my mind I was being the good girl and not being a burden, but as a result my needs were often not met.

A small step towards being you and having a voice can be noticing opportunities to state a preference or how you feel, and experiment with stating what you want. You may not always get your needs met. You may not even get a nice response. But at least you were you. You showed up. You showed to yourself that you and your needs matter, and that it is okay to take up that space.

What about conversations, you may ask. Being vulnerable and bringing yourself into conversations is a key part of meaningful connection. A trap that all of us can fall into when connecting with others while avoiding bringing ourselves into the conversation is the use of gossip or having a common enemy.[68] Gossip involves communication with another, while the target or topic of which is absent or unaware of the communicated content.[69] It is a way of conveying norms of behavior, who is (and isn't) adhering to those norms, and consequences of non-adherence. It is extremely common; in fact, one study found that 90 percent of people engage in gossip in the workplace.[70] In the moment, the action of engaging in gossip makes sense as we can feel like we are connecting with the other person. Yet when you take the gossip or common enemy away, what is there? Does that person really know you? Furthermore, do you feel safe sharing anything personal with them, or are you worried that you will become a topic of gossip for them? As gossip involves conveyance of norms, gossiping can also activate rules around who can and cannot be seen. This can make it harder to hold those rules lightly and show up as ourselves in interactions.

If not connecting through gossip or common enemy, how else can you connect with another person or group? Any way you want, really. If you aren't sure, ask people about themselves. Explore who they are, and what is important to them. Remember to bring yourself into the conversation. If there are similarities, connect and share over them. If there are differences, explore with curiosity.

Notice your environment

Feeling connected to what is important to you and your worth, being open to being seen, and taking steps towards connecting with others, does not mean that you will always have great and meaningful connections. There will be times when the bid for connection will not be reciprocated. There will be times that you encounter people who may not respond nicely to you. It will hurt, and you will be okay.

Having a community, or some people in your corner, can help you be okay and feel like you belong, even when things go awry. Yet those people are not going to magically appear and make you feel welcomed. Your actions of being open to being seen, looking up, and having a voice can help you find them, as can being aware of your environment. What I mean by this is start by going to places that help you connect with your true self. In doing that, you not only will be more likely to connect with you, but also to be around people who have similar values and interests. It creates a safe space for you to experiment with bringing yourself into interactions more. Seek out environments and people that nourish the you that you want to be.

Summary

To belong is to be seen, but if we aren't clear and connected to who we are and our worth, we don't allow ourselves to be seen. Instead, we may go into hiding, or try to fix ourselves so that one day we will fit in and belong. Actions of changing our appearance or who we are are often misguided attempts to belong. In learning how to connect with who we are and to let go of our grip on previously held thoughts and feelings that would get in the way of being seen, we can open ourselves up to making authentic connections one small step at a time. This moves us closer to feeling a sense of belonging in our connections. Rather than changing our bodies to fit in, we show up as we are.

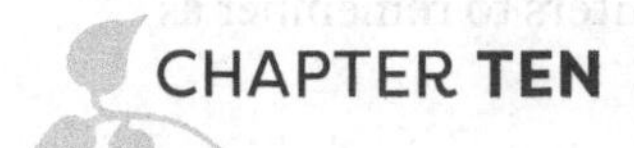

CHAPTER **TEN**

Get Moving!

When we first met in the forest, way back at the beginning of the book, the forest was dark and very powerful, with body image trees and vines that would hold you back from living the life you want to live. Within the forest lurked scary emotion monsters that you would run from or battle with, often at the expense of other things in your life. It was a place where you felt alone and like you would never belong anywhere.

Now, here we are, many chapters later. Those trees and vines may still be thorny and get in the way, but they aren't as powerful. You can unhook from them, step around them, and move towards what is meaningful to you. Those big scary monsters are actually signposts, providing you with information about what is important to you and what you need. With darkness and power of the forest lifting, you can start to move more. The more you move, the more you realize ways that you can move, and that there is more to the forest than the weight and body image trees. You can dictate your story of how you move around and interact with the forest.

The forest has opened up. Pathways, trees, features, things you may not have seen before because the weight and body image trees were blocking them, now come into view. As the forest opens, light streams through hitting you on your face. You can feel its warmth. As you stand there in its warmth you connect with you. There is so much more to you than your body and your weight. You belong, flaws and all. Those thoughts and stories that have held you back from connecting with others and the world may have protected you in the past, but they aren't helpful now. It's time to stop waiting. It is time to live. There is too much to see, and do, and too little time to wait for something as arbitrary as weight.

A few things to remember before taking action

While the forest has transformed, it doesn't mean that everything will be perfect and go smoothly. Hence, there are a few pointers to remember as you embrace your freedom to explore the forest.

You will make mistakes and fail

At some point as you change what you see and do in the forest, you will trip and stumble, *and* you have the power to turn that trip into a funny story, a dance or something else. At times I have perfectionist tendencies. I like to be prepared. I hate looking like an idiot in front of others. I hate failing. I definitely hate others seeing my failures. So much of my life has been focused on preventing mistakes and failure, or at least preventing others from seeing them. Considering this, signing up for an improv class was a push outside my comfort zone.

Our instructor brought our attention to how at some point in the four weeks of classes, we will fail. Our mind will go blank, *and* it won't matter (particularly in the context of a class), *and* some of the most interesting, funny, and creative moments can be born out of those moments. It was a message of you will fail, so try to fail joyfully. Even in the first class, as we all got more comfortable with failing, we loosened up. The creativity grew, and so did the sense of connection.

Surprisingly, it was one of many lessons in improv class that can apply to outside of class and in life. Have you ever done something (whether it is just day-to-day activities, or a trip), and everything went perfectly and there were no issues? Imagine telling someone about that time? How long would it take? How would you feel? Would it be an interesting story? What about times when things have gone sideways? When there has been some mistake or failure? Can you think of any of those times? How long would it take to tell the stories of those times? How would it feel to tell the story of that? How would it feel to listen to it?

I love to travel, and I am very privileged to be in the position throughout my life where I have been able to. Nearly *all* my better travel stories involve something not going to plan, something failing in some way, and what has ensued from that. Sometimes it has worked out, and other times it has been a tale of woe. On my trip to Africa, my partner and I went for a walk around a wetland area with a guide. The idea was that we would see the different terrain, and the different wildlife within it. If things had gone perfectly, I may be telling you a story about the different animals we saw and how they behaved. Nice story, but probably very short and not overly exciting or memorable. This walk didn't go perfectly. We saw rain clouds approaching when we started and thought we would either beat the rain, or else the rain wouldn't be too heavy and we would be fine. We continued with our walk, and once we were past the midway point it started to rain. We kept walking, passing a tiny little shelter as we did. The rain got heavier and heavier, and in the distance, we could hear thunder rolling in. Our guide turned us around, and we headed for the shelter. Within the shelter was a family. They welcomed us in. We took shelter with them for close to an hour. They were kind. They made sure we weren't sitting in places where there were leaks, and despite not knowing any English, tried to connect with us through our guide. It was a spontaneous connection of humanity that was beautiful, and we loved it. We wouldn't have got it if things had gone perfectly to plan. It was things not going to plan that brought out the beauty.

When we are terrified of failing, we put so much effort into multiple plans to try to prevent a mistake or failure. We watch things intensely closely, so that the back up plan can be brought into place with minimal disturbance or anyone catching on that things weren't going as intended. Yet in doing this we miss out on gifts that come from the unplanned, the spontaneous, the mistakes, and the failures. When we hide in shame, covering up the mistakes and failures, we miss out on the storytelling, and the potential sense of commonality, connection, and maybe even laughter.

You will suck

Related to the previous point, you may not make mistakes or fail, but you may not be the greatest or best right away either. Your initial different steps around the forest may look like a newborn, or me trying to walk on an icy surface—very shaky and definitely not graceful. And that is okay. You may or may not get better, but you can still take away a sense of achievement of "I did a thing."

I have done silks and trapeze. At the beginning I *really* sucked. When I began, I did not have the core, nor the arm strength, to pull myself into the basic positions. In my first few lessons there were multiple times when I had to be shoved up into position by my coach. There were times that I got tangled in such a way that the tangle, combined with my lack of strength, meant the coach would have to fetch a stool to untangle me and release me from the mess I had created. There is no way of hiding your mistake or failure when it results in you being trapped dangling in the air. In my first performance, I fell out of the hammock in a smooth cartwheel like motion, that surprisingly seemed to have enough element of grace that for a split second the audience thought it was part of the piece and almost expected others to cartwheel out as well. The look of panic on my face and frantic jumping back up probably ruined that illusion. Even after doing aerial for multiple years, I still wasn't all that good. There were countless times I'd find my boobs or other body parts getting in the way. Not to mention all the times I would find myself giggling on the crashmat over how I completely messed up a move resulting in ungraceful dismount. There were many times I could have just focused on how I sucked (and there were times when I did), but when that happened, I lost focus of the things I was enjoying about aerial. Each time I went to class, or did a performance, I was doing things, facing fears, getting stronger and experiencing life.

Keep those compassion and curiosity glasses at hand

Not being good at things, making mistakes and failing aren't easy or fun to experience, yet keeping hold of those compassion and curiosity glasses will help you be kind to yourself when it happens, as well as help you learn ways to keep going that work for you. If you are kind and curious as you take new steps, you will be able to notice if the discomfort is coming from not being good at something, or if it is because you don't have as much interest in it as you thought. In being curious, you will also notice those tiny little gains and moments of growth that happen when you do something new.

An incredible amount of information and movement goes through the elbow. How do I know this? I dislocated it. Not on purpose, but in one of my aerial mishaps resulting in a painful dismount. Throughout the injury recovery journey, I had the compassion and curiosity glasses firmly on. If I hadn't done this, I would have spiralled into attacking myself for the injury and what I was not able to do. I was frustrated by the injury, absolutely, but the shame and self attack spiral was not going to get my arm working again. I curiously noticed just how many movements that I took for granted were impacted by a dislocated elbow. As my elbow started to heal, my curiosity allowed me to notice the very tiny increments of strength returning. They were small, but they helped me do the exercises and things that I needed to do to restore functioning to the elbow. If I hadn't seen them, and just focused on what I couldn't do, I probably wouldn't have been as dedicated to my role in recovery, and I wouldn't have built the appreciation I now have for what the body can do.

Don't believe the highlights reel is the norm

Everyone else at some time in their life has failed and sucked at something. We generally don't shout these moments from the rooftops, flood our socials, or start interviews with them, but we all have those not great times. What we put forward, especially initially, are the highlight reels. The things we have achieved and excel at. Yet this creates an inflated sense of perfection. If all we see is the highlights, our brain assumes that is the norm. It isn't.

In recent years, I have tried to add to the reel that is being shown by sharing what I am experiencing, including if I am being challenged. Before doing this, I assumed people would judge me, look at me with disappointment and disgust and run/walk away. What I have found interesting is the amount of people who look at me with relief, followed by a knowing smile and some variation of "I thought it was just me." Many times, it has created a shift in energy, from people being side by side not smiling and trying to be perfect, to smiling and connecting. The highlight reel is inaccurate, and fighting to maintain it keeps us disconnected and from trying new things.

You don't have to do it on your own

For many years, one of the stories I told myself was, if you wanted something done right, do it yourself. Other people can't be trusted and will only disappoint. This is not accurate. Sure, if you ask the wrong person, or there is a mismatch between what you are asking and what someone is capable of giving, there may be disappointment. But often people are open to helping and providing support, especially if you are clear on what you need. As you think about taking steps, and doing things differently, think about what you may need from others. Are you needing encouragement? Are you needing them to come with you when you do something for the first time? Are you needing accountability? Once you are clear on what you need, think who in your life may be most suited to providing that need. If you can, have multiple people, as sometimes for whatever reason a person may say no. Then, ask.

While my name is on this book, I have not been alone in writing it. I have people around me who I have turned to depending on what I am needing. Sometimes I reached out to the Contextual Behavioural Science Community to bounce ideas and get inspired. Sometimes I turned to my colleagues where I work for support, guidance, and ideas. Sometimes I turned to my loved ones for encouragement and support to help me ride through the waves of self doubt. Has it been hard at times to ask? Yes. Have there been times when people weren't able to give what I needed? Yes. And I survived it.

Basically, you will suck and fail, so be compassionate and curious with yourself. You aren't alone in the struggles and people are there to help if you let them.

Taking action

It can be helpful to set goals when taking action. A goal is something that you would like to achieve. Value-based goals are those which you would like to achieve within the broad area of a value. For example, you may value knowledge, and therefore you may set a goal of completing a course.

When thinking about setting goals, our minds can jump to big or longer-term goals. This isn't bad, it gives us something to shoot for, but if we aren't plotting steps along the way we run off getting overwhelmed or disheartened when we have been working hard, but not there yet. If we think of goals like distances, living in Eastern Canada and having family in Western Australia, I can set the goal of getting to my family, but there isn't a direct flight from where I am, to my hometown. I need multiple steps to get there. The long-term goal of home has to be broken into the shorter-term goal of another location (usually in Canada or US), and another medium-term goal location (usually in Asia). The direction I am heading, south, is like my values, and the goals/stops along the way are letting me know I am heading in the right direction.

When setting values-based goals it can be helpful to think about big goals within your values. Then break that into smaller pieces. Steps that, when you achieve them, would let you know you are moving closer to the bigger goal. Think big, if weight and body image weren't taking up as much space, and you were fully connected with what is important to you, what would you like to be doing or achieving? Now break that into small steps.

For some people, thinking big and then breaking into small steps is too overwhelming and doesn't fit with how their brain works. I know sometimes when I think big, it creates space for the self doubt monster to come in and shut the door on my idea. Sometimes going the other direction can be helpful, as it allows you to have a few wins and build your confidence before taking on the bigger goals. What I mean when I say going the other direction is, instead of starting big and breaking into pieces, instead start really small and build. When I say small, I mean really small. If you have perfectionist tendencies this may be a challenge, as your brain will tell you the small step is too small and thus doesn't matter or isn't worth doing. Think of one of your values and think of the smallest possible step you could take that would be consistent with it.

It is important that when you are setting the goals that they are focused on what is within your control. You may value connection and set the goal of being in an intimate relationship. Yet you can't control who may enter your life, and how they may respond to you. But you can set the goal of going on more dates or going on a dating app or website.

It can also be helpful to write the goals down, and if possible, have a realistic timeline. When doing different activities in my life I may have an idea of a possible goal or something I would like to do, and I am really excited. If I don't write it down, I forget. Sometimes it reappears, and sometimes not. Writing it down also holds me accountable, especially if I have set a timeline and have told others about the timeline. It is important to be realistic and flexible with the timeline. Life can be messy, and other demands on you may change over time and change your ability to be able to pursue the goal in the way you intended to. If you aren't realistic with the timeline, you will soon find yourself overwhelmed and stress. Trust me. Been there, done that.

SELF-REFLECTION MOMENT: SMALL STEPS TO VALUES

- What were your values?
- Think big. Reflecting on your values, if weight and body image wasn't taking up as much space in your life, what would you be doing and achieving?
- Are there smaller pieces or goals within that big picture that you can set and move towards?
- Start small. Reflecting on your values, what is the smallest possible thing you could do today or this week that would be consistent with your values?
- Are there steps that may be easier to take once you have taken that first one? How could you build on that at your own pace?

Keep going

Sadly, I have lost a number of people in my life. Many people when faced with the death of a loved one pause and reflect on their own life. They take stock and think about what is important to them. This can lead to their priorities shifting, and to them setting intentions and promises to do things differently. At that moment, they are passionate and mean it. This is important to them. They may say they will connect with loved ones more. Be more authentic, and open. Not sweat the small stuff. Maybe say that they will have a healthier lifestyle to try to evade their own mortality. Yet, return a year or more later, and many of the intents and promises are no longer being fulfilled. Not because they didn't want to, or it wasn't important, but because change is hard.

SELF-REFLECTION MOMENT: PAST BARRIERS TO SUSTAINING CHANGE

Think of your own relationship with change. Bring to mind times when you tried to do something different or form a new habit.

- Were you able to sustain it? If so, what helped you keep going?
- If you weren't able to sustain it, what happened? Did you quit when obstacles were encountered? Did you gradually lose steam, and the behavior became less and less frequent?
- What thoughts did you have or stories that you told yourself?
- Is this how you would like to engage in change in your life? If not, what would you rather see yourself doing?

Your past experiences in relation to change can provide information about what you may encounter the next time you try new things or change. If it happened in the past, there is a chance it will happen again. You can use these past reflections, to help anticipate future obstacles and decide how you want to respond next time.

If you are someone who quits or goes into hiding when obstacles are encountered, how do you want to respond when you encounter obstacles? You may not know what obstacles you will encounter, but you can set an intention of how you would like to respond to them. What may you need to help you respond in your intended way to obstacles? Are you needing to defuse from your thoughts or story? Are you needing help in taking action in the presence of emotions? Are you needing the support of others?

If you are someone for whom the change just runs out of steam, and you do things less and less frequently until it becomes nonexistent again, how do you want to respond when you notice the frequency dropping? Again, what do you need to help you in that response?

SELF-REFLECTION MOMENT: TACKLING FUTURE BARRIERS

- What do you tend to do when trying to create change?
- What would you like to do?
- How would you like to respond when you see old patterns creeping back (such as quitting or losing steam)?
- What do you need to help you respond in that way?

Time for bigger change in the forest

Your forest and how you move through it may be changing, but that doesn't mean you won't ever find yourself brought up by the body image trees and vines. They are still in your forest. You are just more equipped to choose what you do when you encounter them. Those experiences that helped the body image trees in your forest grow are still at play, and as long as they are, those trees will continue to grow and threaten to take over the whole forest. There are many out there who are trapped in the forest, and there are many more that will continue to be trapped over time. Until we take action at a bigger level, those climate forces will continue. Your limbs are free now, not tangled or restricted by the foliage of the forest. You can use this newfound movement to create change to help others.

PART **FOUR**

NAVIGATING THE FOREST FOR OTHERS

CHAPTER **ELEVEN**

Change the Dialogues

To protect ourselves and others from getting stuck in the forest, we need change beyond our own internal experiences. We need change at the level of how we interact and treat each other, and beyond. What might seem like small acts of kindness or compassion between people can push a person along a path of feeling a sense of safety or belonging. Conversely, what may seem like a small act, like a look or an unkind word, can push a person into a spiral of feeling judged, alone and not good enough. A simple micro-reaction can send someone into hiding or fighting, or entice them to come out, take up space and shine. What is wonderful is that we have the power to choose and shape the direction it goes. We don't always have to do big things to create change at a bigger level. Small changes in the day-to-day interactions we have can make a difference, and interrupt some of the climate forces that are currently nurturing the body image trees

Micro acts of kindness

I had to go shopping for a dress for a formal event. I am not someone who enjoys shopping, yet there I was in the mall looking for a dress, dragging my partner along for moral support, to snap me out of an internal spiral or placate my ranting or both. There were two stores that stood out and they captured the impact of seemingly small differences in action. At the first store, the woman behind the counter gave me the up and down look, which was followed by a slight curl of the lip of disgust. Many of you may know this look that I speak of. It is a sizing up and is often then followed by an expression of approval or disapproval. Today it was disapproval. I assume my body and my attire failed the test to be acceptable to stand in this store. To be on the receiving end of this is not fun. It can feel like you are in the schoolyard again and being picked on or excluded. In that split second, I could feel my body start to curl in, and I wanted to shrink away and not be seen.

In the second store, I was not met with an up and down look. I was met with a smile. When I stepped out of the changeroom, I did not receive a look of judgment of my body. I was met with a noticing of the dress and the color and whether the fit suited or didn't suit me. Suggestions of possible alterations to improve comfort and suitability for occasions were made in a helpful manner, and not in a way that could create shame for needing them. I felt seen and respected. It was nice.

The experience in each of these stores and how it made me feel was very different. My appearance and body didn't change between them, but I got very different interactions. The first store I felt like I didn't belong. I felt like I should be ashamed for even thinking of setting foot in there. How dare I let myself be seen?!? While in the second store, I felt good being seen.

That is all it takes to take a step towards making a person feel welcome, an acknowledgment of their presence by turning towards them or making eye contact and an authentic warm smile. Imagine entering a room where you don't know anyone and are feeling nervous. What happens to those nerves when you catch eyes with someone, and something about their expression or body language is peaceful and welcoming?

When reflecting on my life, the lives of those around me, and in listening to my clients, I have noticed that we each hold something very powerful, and that is the power to influence how people around us feel. An expression, comment, or action, which is seemingly insignificant, can make someone feel really good, or sad, or angry. When people are reflecting on a person's life after they passed, they often share stories of how that person made them feel. In any interaction you have with another person, whether there are words involved or not, you can make a person feel something. So, ask yourself, how do I want to make others feel? Then ask, what is the smallest thing I can do to help them feel that (either verbally or nonverbally) and try to do that more. This doesn't mean you have to do it with every interaction. That may be exhausting or feel inauthentic. You may not feel like you have it in you to give a gift in every interaction. Yet many people find that when they do these micro acts of kindness and see the reaction in another person, they want to keep doing it. It doesn't feel like a chore. It feels like warmth that is spread from one person to another. These small acts convey to another person that no matter what they look like they matter and deserve to feel connection and belonging.

Interrupting unhelpful acts

It can be uplifting to look at the small acts we can take in each interaction to spread kindness and try to offset the rampant and damaging weight stigma. Yet, that only goes so far and, at some point, we need to look at the hurtful and harmful things ourselves and those around us are doing that perpetuate weight stigma. It can be an uncomfortable process, yet it is in service of making the world a better place for all, not just those who meet an arbitrary set of standards of appearance.

As someone who has been working in the field of eating disorders and body image for over 15 years, I would love to be able to say that all my actions throughout my life have been consistent with the messages I convey in this book. But they haven't. I am a human, who like you wants to belong, and has also been exposed to the societal messages that link belonging to appearance.

Not only are we provided with ample messages about how we have to look a certain way to belong, but also that we have to engage in appearance related interactions. In our youth there is the presence of "fat talk." Over time we branch beyond fat talk and move towards broader conversations about our own and other people's weight and body, as well as diets. These kinds of conversations are so common, they have become part of normal social discourse which creates a sense of pressure to engage in them for connection and belonging.

I draw attention to the yearning for connection and belonging that can drive these actions, not as an excuse or to condone or say the actions are okay, but rather to draw attention to how the actions make sense. In seeing that it makes sense, shaming and blaming can somewhat be eased, thus making it easier to look at unhelpful or hurtful actions that we may have engaged in.

For the longest time I would not look at the past actions or inactions

I did that I know contributed to the perpetuation of weight stigma. I felt so much guilt and shame. I would pretend the actions didn't happen so I could avoid those feelings. I justified avoiding looking at my actions by assuming that, as I know and understand more now, I would automatically behave better. While there were improvements, particularly around anything more overt (such as, you will not hear me comment on a person's weight), I still would find myself floundering with more subtle interactions or responding when other people are engaging in body talk.

One particularly shameful memory I have was a time when I was at a pub with my then boyfriend and his friends. A fat woman walked in, and he made a fat joke and he and his mates all laughed. I sat in silence. I did nothing. He had said the joke loud enough that the woman could hear it. I watched her face drop, and her eyes look down. She was trying to shrink away. I did nothing. Nothing to comfort her or let her know I was an ally and did not agree with the behavior. Nothing to tell my boyfriend and his friends that those actions were so cruel. My inaction was an action that condoned weight stigma. This kind of inaction and the pain it caused another was something I tried to pretend didn't happen.

It was only when I softened my stance towards myself could I then hold my guilt and look at these actions and learn so that I don't make the mistakes again. My action and inaction are responses that I no longer am comfortable with, as this (the fight against the climate of weight stigma) is too important. The people being hurt by it are too incredible to be shunted into the shadows of the forest.

I invite you to look at the hard stuff and feel the discomfort that comes with it, because only in doing so can we create change. Yet as you look at the actions, I encourage you to provide yourself and those around you with compassion. Remember the actions that you see are just that: actions. They are not who you are. And in looking at the actions, you are creating space to learn, and choose a different action. Remind yourself that the actions you took are a product of your conditioning. This doesn't mean you are okay or happy with the action, but rather you are acknowledging that they make sense given the information you held at that time. You have gathered more information since then, and the actions you would take now may be different. The fact that you are feeling discomfort indicates that there is something there that is important to you.

SELF-REFLECTION MOMENT: AWARENESS OF PAST HURT

Take a moment, think about whether you or the people around you have done any of the following;

- Made a comment to another about their weight (regardless of whether it is positive or negative). For example, "Wow, you look like you have lost weight."
- Made assumptions about a person's activity level based on their weight.
- Reacted to someone differently because of their weight.
- Made comments about a person's clothing and their weight (for example, "They shouldn't wear that outfit at that size").
- Made judgment about a person's food selections based on their weight.
- Made a comment to other people about a person's weight (for example, "Did you see Jenny, it looks like she has gained weight").
- Changed your interactions with someone based on their weight.
- Engaged in conversations about dieting.
- Not come to a person's defence when comments about their weight were made.
- Made a joke about weight.
- Laughed at a joke about weight.
- Made assumptions about a person's health based on their weight.
- Given a person the up and down look.
- Not come to a person's defence when comments were made about their clothing and weight.
- Other: ....

Take a moment, for each of those items you noted you have engaged in, reflect on how you were thinking and feeling when it happened. Was it part of social interaction? Did it feel part of the natural flow of conversation? Did it feel like a way of connecting with others? Did it feel uncomfortable, like something you should or shouldn't say or do, but you were not sure what else to do? Was it coming from a self-preservation place, to stay connected to the group or protect self from comment or attack? Was it a means of pushing another person down, to lift yourself up? Did it just happen, with no real thought or intent?

Then reflect and notice what thoughts and feelings come up for you right now as you reflect on these times. Are you sad? Do you feel guilty? Are you angry at yourself? Are there thoughts of "I should" or "I shouldn't have?" Are there no thoughts or feelings?

If you could turn back time, and go back to those instances, would you do anything differently? If not, why not? If so, what would you do and why, and what would help you do something differently?

AWARENESS OF PAST HURT

What was the hurtful action that you identified:

....

....

....

....

What was happening within you at the time that moved you closer to that action?

....

....

....

....

Any emotions emerging as you reflect on the action, and the things that may have contributed to you taking the action?

....

....

....

....

If you could turn back time, and go back to that instance, would you do anything differently? If not, why not? If so, what would you do and why, and what would help you do something differently?

....

....

....

....

Changing the dialogue at different levels

That can be a hard exercise to do. It can bring up guilt, shame, frustration, and anger. Yet the reflections can give insight to how you want to act in the future, and things you might want to do differently. So, let us dig into that a little more.

The items on that list fall into three groups:

- *Internal* are your own thoughts, including judgment or assumptions
- *Actions* are the actions that you did, such as making comments or treating people differently
- *Responses* are actions that occur around you in relation to weight, and your response to these.

You can be involved in change at one, two, or all three levels.

Internal: Your thoughts and judgments towards others

Our minds are programmed to think, so we are going to have thoughts emerge all the time. Our minds also have all these lovely shortcuts to help us process information. Often our assumptions and judgments are a product of these shortcuts, combined with the environment we live in. As a result, thoughts may pop up, even though we don't like them or agree with them. It does not make us bad people. We may not be able to choose what thoughts pop up and when, but we can choose what we do next.

Let us take a few moments to think about possible different ways of responding to the thoughts, and their impact. As we go through the different responses, I am going to share some of my experiences of responding in different ways, not to try to convince you of how to respond, but rather to give you an idea of what you might see.

One way to respond to the thoughts that pop up is to believe the thoughts and see them as important truths. How would that impact your actions? For example, how would you react to another person if you truly believed the thought "someone that weight shouldn't be wearing that."

When I think of times that I have bought into the thought, I have treated the person consistent with that judgment, and used assumptions to justify it. I am the least proud of actions I take when I respond to some of my thoughts in that way. Thankfully this occurs infrequently now, as I have actively worked on this piece.

Another response to the thoughts may be to try to argue or challenge the thought. For example, in response to assumptions of health in relation to weight, you may argue back with "a person's weight doesn't always indicate their health. There are plenty of people who fall in the normal weight range who are unhealthy, and there are plenty of people who fall in the overweight range who are healthy." How might responding to your thoughts by challenging them or coming up with an alternate perspective impact your thoughts, feelings, and actions?

I know when I have responded to my thoughts in this way, sometimes it has been helpful. It has led to me getting perspective and adjusting the original thought. Other times, particularly if I am in a stubborn or irritable place, I argue back. A battle erupts in my head, with each side bringing different information, or just doubling down on its original position. Just as evidence opposing the thought builds, so does evidence that supports it. While the battle plays out in my head, I am not very present at all to the world around me.

Another way of responding might be attacking yourself for having the thought. For example, you might have a judgment about what a person is wearing and their weight, and you catch yourself and think "That was really mean. You are such a ..." How might that impact how you feel and the actions you take?

For me, if I am irritable, my thoughts aren't nice, and my brain doesn't discriminate in its attacks, everyone is fair game (including myself). During these times, not nice and unhelpful thoughts do tend to pop up, and it wouldn't be unusual for that to then be used as ammunition against myself: "Wow, what kind of mean person are you for thinking that, and you work in mental health! You should know better!" I then sink into some guilt and shame, and shrink away from interacting with people, which I justify as protecting them from me.

Yet another way of responding to the thought, is to notice it, acknowledge it and unhook from it. You might say, "Ah there is that tree again" or "That is my conditioning talking." How might that way of responding impact your feelings and your actions?

For me, when I respond to my thoughts in this way I get less caught up in thoughts and feelings, and I can connect with the present and my values more. Usually, the actions I take from this stance are ones I am prouder of.

You can think of responses to your thoughts being like a choose your own adventure story. Next time a thought pops up, experiment with how you respond to it and notice where the story goes. How does it impact how you think, feel and act? If it is a story arc that you like, then go back to it. If it is one you don't like, choose a different path next time.

CHOOSE YOUR OWN ADVENTURE

Internal experience: thoughts and feelings	Response to it (for example, believed it, challenged it, defused it)	What happened?	Would you take that path again? Why? Why not?

Actions: Your actions towards others

When you were looking at your thoughts, the actions probably popped up as well, because they are often connected to your thoughts. You may be more or less likely to behave in a certain way based on the thoughts you are having. For example, if you are having thoughts of negative judgment of someone, you may be more likely to dismiss or be rude to them.

Actions are things that you initiate, or you engage in. Take a moment to have a look at the actions list below and notice any that you frequently or recently engaged in. If there are others that aren't listed that you have engaged in, add them to the list.

- Made a comment to another about their weight (regardless of whether it is positive or negative).
- Reacted to someone differently because of their weight.
- Made comments about a person's clothing and their weight (for example, "They shouldn't wear that outfit at that size").
- Made a comment to other people about a person's weight (for example, "Did you see Jenny, it looks like she has gained weight").

- Changed your interactions with someone based on their weight.
- Engaged in conversations about dieting.
- Made a joke or laughed at a joke about weight.
- Given a person the up and down look.
- Other: ....

Take a moment now and reflect on the values you identified earlier in Part Two of this book. Connect with those values for a moment, and ask yourself: if those values were directing my behaviors how would I behave in that situation? An answer that may come to mind is, "I wouldn't make the comment/joke/action." If you weren't making the comment/joke/action, what would you do instead? Would you connect with the person? If so, how would you connect with them?

When I think of my values of connection, kindness, and compassion, and ask those questions, the first thing that pops into my mind is "I wouldn't do that." What I would do instead would vary depending on the situation. If it was an interaction with a stranger, if I was behaving consistently with my values, I would make eye contact, smile, and say hello. If it was someone I know, then I would move towards connecting with who they are and what is happening in their life, as opposed to anything about their weight.

Take a moment to go back through the list of actions item by item identifying the ones that you tend to do or have done recently and ask whether that action is consistent or inconsistent with your values and the you that you want to be. If the behaviors are inconsistent, try to hold yourself with compassion, and think of how you would rather handle the situation. What action would be more consistent with your values? It may feel tedious to go through the action list in this way, but chances are if these situations have occurred frequently in the past, they are likely to occur in the future. Thinking and planning now, prevents you from having to think on your feet, and reduces the risk of falling back into old, conditioned patterns.

CHANGE ACTIONS TOWARDS OTHERS

Look at the list and place a mark next to items that you have done recently or frequently do.

- ☐ Made a comment to another about their weight (regardless of whether it is positive or negative).
- ☐ Reacted to someone differently because of their weight.
- ☐ Made comments about a person's clothing and their weight (for example, "They shouldn't wear that at that size").
- ☐ Made a comment to other people about a person's weight (for example, "Did you see Jenny, it looks like she has gained weight").
- ☐ Changed your interactions with someone based on their weight.
- ☐ Engaged in conversations about dieting.
- ☐ Made a joke or laughed at a joke about weight.
- ☐ Given a person the up and down look.
- ☐ Other: ....
- ☐ Other: ....

Reflect on your values. Are the actions consistent or inconsistent with who you want to be?

....

....

What alternate actions would you take that would be more consistent with your values?

....

Is there anything that would help you take that alternate action?

....

Responses: Your response to other people's actions

Move now to your responses when another person engages in unhelpful or hurtful comments and actions. Notice, out of the list below, items that you frequently or recently witnessed or were a part of. If there are others that come to mind, then add them to the list.

- Heard someone make a comment to another person about their weight (for example, "You look like you have lost weight").
- Witnessed someone treat another person differently because of their weight (for example, talked over them or rolled their eyes at them, overlooking them to give someone else their full attention).
- Heard others make comments about a person's clothing and their weight.
- Had a person make comments to you about another person's weight (for example, "Did you see Jenny? It looks like she has gained weight").
- Been in or around conversations about dieting.
- Heard a joke about weight.
- Laughed at a joke about weight.
- Other: ....

Think about how you responded when these situations unfolded. Did you ignore the comment or action? Did you challenge it? Did you come to the person's defence? Did you then engage in it? Did you try to change the topic? Did you leave?

Again, now take a moment to connect with your values and who you want to be. Then ask, is my response consistent with my values? If the responses are inconsistent, then gently move your thoughts to ways of responding that may be more consistent with your values. You may want to come up with a couple of options, as sometimes you may not be able to do the response that is most consistent with your values (for a variety of reasons).

Many people don't engage in actions consistent with their values because of fear, particularly if it involves more confrontational forms of responding (for example, telling someone that the comment was not appropriate). Sadly, we live in a world where sometimes that fear is justified. If that is the case, then explore alternate responses. Do the next best thing, so that you can act consistently with your values and protect yourself. For example, if the person making an inappropriate comment towards one of your coworkers in a meeting was your boss, you may be fearful that if you say something in the meeting your boss could fire, harass, or bully you. Instead of speaking out in the meeting you may go to your coworker after the meeting and provide support.

Sometimes, we experience fear and there isn't a significant threat present. For example, a comment may be made among friends or acquaintances. You are not likely to lose your job for speaking out, but there may be people who have a different opinion to you, and they may not agree with you. In these situations, you may feel torn, as multiple values may be compromised, and regardless of which action you take a part of you becomes threatened. In these situations, you may ask yourself what response is the most liveable, or would make me proud?

There may be times when having a voice (even though the fear is there) is the option you choose, and there may be other times that that may not be possible, and you move towards doing the next best thing consistent with your values. "If I can't have a voice, I am going to at least be there for that person." Whatever it is, choose to do something different. Choose to not be part of the problem that keeps people trapped in the forest.

CHANGE THE RESPONSE

Look at the list and place a mark next to items that you have recently experienced or frequently experience.

- ☐ Heard someone make a comment to another person about their weight (for example, "You look like you have lost weight").
- ☐ Witnessed someone treat another person differently because of their weight (for example, talked over them or rolled their eyes at them, overlooking them to give someone else their full attention).
- ☐ Heard others make comments about a person's clothing and weight.

- ☐ Had a person make comments to you about another person's weight (for example, "Did you see Jenny? It looks like she has gained weight").
- ☐ Been in or around conversations about dieting.
- ☐ Heard a joke about weight.
- ☐ Laughed at a joke about weight.
- ☐ Other: ....
- ☐ Other: ....

Reflect on your values. Are the actions consistent or inconsistent with who you want to be?

....

....

How would you want to respond to the situation that would be more consistent with your values?

....

....

Is there anything that would help you take that alternate action?

....

....

Ripples in a pond

Whether you are changing your response to your thoughts, your actions, or how you respond to others, a little can go a long way. When you throw a stone in a pond, even if it is a very small stone, the point of impact ripples out and causes change over a bigger area of that pond. Your actions, no matter how small, are similar, they have a ripple effect, and who knows how far your ripple will go.

RIPPLE VISUALIZATION

Imagine you are sitting by a small pond. The water is still. It is so still, that the surface acts like a mirror. Clearly reflecting the sky above. There are several stones or pebbles around where you are seated. You pick one up and throw it into the pond. You watch as it hits the water. Then you notice the ripples of that impact spreading outwards in the pond. Your actions have ripples. Imagine holding a door open for someone who is struggling. You make eye contact with them and give them a friendly, comforting smile. You may even say something funny or kind that makes them smile. Imagine, that moment changed that person's day. Prior to that moment they had multiple little things go wrong, including people being rude to them, and now they are in a rush and frustrated and irritated with people in general. That moment with you at the door was the first bit of kindness they had all day. It was the first time they smiled all day. They may have had the thought "maybe people aren't that bad," and their mood shifted just a little bit. A ripple. That same person then goes to get a coffee, they place their order, and the server makes a mistake. Instead of yelling at them like they may have done earlier when they were more irritable, they are kind and compassionate in their response. Imagine the server, who has had a busy shift, as it is a busy day, and the store is a couple of staff short. Because it is so busy, they have made a couple of mistakes during the day, the last was just a moment ago, and the person had yelled and berated them. They are feeling tired, flustered, defeated, and wanting to quit. Having a kind and compassionate response to a mistake feels like a breath of fresh air and helps them get through their shift. Another ripple. And the ripples keep going. Think of a time when you had a moment of kindness or compassion with another, or when you stood up and protected them, or when you comforted them when they were hurt. Then take a moment to think of what ripples may have come from that one little moment, with that one person. We may never find out how far our ripples may travel, but we definitely won't find out if we don't cast a stone and make an impact. What impact do you want to make?

A guided audio version of this can be found online at www.jkp.com/catalogue/book/9781839977237.

CHAPTER **TWELVE**

Help the Youth

Ripples from your actions will be seen by and impact the youth and future generations. Yet big change takes time, and sadly the youth of today will encounter similar messages and challenges to those we have experienced. As much as we may want to bundle the youth up and protect them from the trees and thorns within the forest, it isn't possible. In helping the youth, we need to begin with helping build their resilience to when they encounter painful or hurtful messages, as well as build their ability to celebrate body diversity and not engage in actions that support weight stigma.

Help kids navigate the forest

Before we can look at helping our youth create change, we need to begin with helping them navigate the forest.

Be the person you needed

One of my favourite proverbs, often misattributed to Mahatma Gandhi, is "Be the change you want to see in the world." When looking at body image and helping the future generations, I twist it a little bit to "Be the person you needed when you had your struggles." Let's dig into how to identify what that could be.

Take a moment, and notice what are some of your most challenging/daunting trees or vines in the forest. What thoughts or stories grab you the quickest and hardest and bring you to a complete stop? Can you remember when they, or a variation of them, first started to appear? I say variation, because as a child you may not have had the same words to capture what was in your mind and body. How old were you when these thoughts or stories first appeared?

My mind goes back to a number of memories when I was very young, and they all have the same theme. I was excited about something and wanted to step into the spotlight. The times when I was excited about an outfit that I wanted to wear, or times where I had a creative story that I wanted to bring to play or write. Times when I had achieved something and wanted to share my success. Amid these moments of excitement I came across someone laughing at me, scorning me for wanting the spotlight or pushing me aside because someone or something was better. These experiences birthed, the "I'm not good enough, and not worthy of being seen" story. Later, when forming friendships and schoolyard crushes, this story would gain more depth to it, with appearance beginning to be weaved in. I recall being in my teens and approaching a crush, only to be informed that they preferred girls with a different body type.

This was little me, starting to see the darkness, and get lost in the forest. Little me was too quiet, not smart enough, not pretty enough, just not enough to belong in the spotlight. So, she hid in the dark recesses of the forest. If you can't see me, you can't see my flaws.

For many years, I struggled to look at that younger me because I had bought so much into the stories that the world around me had curated, and I had come to tell myself. I continued to add to the list of all the ways she was not good enough. I thought little me was quiet, ugly, stupid, should've known how to be better, and, worst of all, was selfish. I thought she deserved to be stuck in the forest because she was such a self-absorbed little brat. Now I look at her differently, and see what shaped her, and her innocence. If I had the power to go back in time and visit that girl, I would hug her and tell her not to let go of her excitement or her creativity. I'd tell her that she is unique, and similar at the same time. That, while some people may laugh and criticize her uniqueness, others will appreciate it. I am grateful that my mother at times would do this, and she would role model keeping on going with what you enjoy, even if others find it odd and laugh.

I see kids now appearing to get lost in the darker parts of the forest. I think about the kinds of people who were helpful when I was their age or what I needed then, and I strive to be that. I won't be able to protect them from the world, but I can let them know that I see them for who they are, accept them, and will be a safe space for them. I want to role model that they can be different and find joy in that, even though others may not always appreciate it.

Think about the young you, when the thoughts that plague you now first started to appear. What were you needing from those around you? When you think of the adults around you at the time, what did you need from them? Is that a response you can enact in your interactions with people now? When you think of your peers around you at that time, what did you need from them? Is it a response you would like to teach others?

BE THE PERSON YOU NEEDED

When did you first get impacted by the body image trees?

....

....

What was happening, and what did the trees look like?

....

....

What did that young you need from the adults around you at that time?

....

....

Can you use that information to guide how you act now? If so, how?

....

....

What did that young you need from your peers around you at that time?

....

....

Can you use that information to guide how you teach youth to behave? If so, how?

....

....

Sit with them through the pain

If you are a parent, there likely will be times when your child will come to you with experiences of being teased or shunned because of appearance, whether it is what they weigh, are wearing, their skin, or how they express their gender. When this happens, don't dismiss them or tell them it doesn't matter, or it is silly. In that moment they are hurting, and what might not seem like a big deal to us as adults, in their child or teen world is a very big deal. You may not be able to take their pain away. You may not be able to fix it, but you can be with them and provide comfort as they go through it. You can also provide reassurance that the pain they feel in that moment will pass, and even if it is replaced by another pain or hurt, they have so much to give the world and experience. The pain will happen, and so will so much more.

To this day, I don't recall the details of what was happening other than it was one of my first teen heartbreak experiences, but I do recall my mother's response. I curled up next to my mum and was sobbing. The cry that comes from deep within making it hard to breathe. My mum hugged me. She told me she knew it hurt a lot in that moment, but it wouldn't always feel that way. She didn't promise that I would never feel that way again, quite the opposite, she said there will be other times that I will feel that way *and* that as much as they hurt, I would get through it, and she will always love me and be there. Though it wasn't exactly what I wanted to hear at that moment, it was what I needed to hear. It didn't stop my tears from flowing then, but it helped me get through the ones that would follow.

You belong as you are

We have all received the messages conveying what you have to look like and do in order to belong. We have likely all at times felt like we don't belong. It is painful. Yet the intensity of the pain is increased when that sense of not belonging, or having to meet a set of criteria in order to belong, is felt at home.

We want the best for kids, which is great. Yet it can lead to some ways of interacting that may come from an encouraging intent but may be heard or experienced as conditional love. Many of you reading this book may be children of exercise or diet families. The encouragement and praise experienced around diet and weight loss, can send the message of "I will be loved if I am good—diet, exercise and lose weight." Our brains, being what they are, also learn "If I am not dieting, exercising, or losing weight I am bad, and not loved." All of a sudden, something that may have come from good intent has removed a sense of love and belonging at home.

I was lucky in my home. I didn't experience this in relation to diet, exercise, and weight, but I did experience it in relation to grades. It created an intense pressure on me to do well and worries when I didn't do well, or as well as some of my peers. This pressure exploded in the car in my teens one day. After I shared my grade (which was a good one), and my mother's first response was asking how that grade was compared to someone else. I erupted into tears and anger, as in that moment it felt like receiving love and praise was not only dependent on whether I did well overall, but whether I did better than someone else. Once the wave of emotions passed, my mum and I could have a more reasonable discussion about my experience and we talked through it, but prior to that point getting grades back was highly distressing for me. It wasn't about the grade itself; it was whether I would be accepted and loved if the grade was low or not as good as others.

Building a sense of belonging at home, doesn't mean you stop encouraging actions out of fear it will be heard as conditional love. It is about encouraging children *and* letting them know that regardless of what happens they still matter and are still loved. As we live in an appearance-focused world, they are getting enough messages about appearance the second they leave the door or pick up a device. In the home, you get to see so much more. You get to see their sense of humor, their quirks, their creativity, their intelligence, their compassion, and their flaws. By drawing attention to what makes them who they are, you are providing messaging that they are more than their appearance.

Work together to change the climate

So far, we have looked at helping the youth by creating a safe space and helping them through the challenges of the current appearance-focused climate that is full of weight stigma. This can create a degree of change, yet we want the youth to go beyond that. We want them to be part of bigger climate change, shaping a world where there is less appearance-based discrimination. To do that, we need to provide information that will help them be able to interact differently.

Unpicking the assumptions underlying weight stigma

The presence of weight stigma and discrimination nurtures the growth of the body image trees. Thus, reducing the presence of weight stigma and discrimination should help stunt the growth of the trees that can be problematic in the forest. There are three key assumptions associated with weight that contribute to weight stigma and discrimination:

- A certain weight or shape is desirable, and thus anything outside of that range is bad.
- A person's weight is an indicator of their health.
- A person's weight is controllable.

By having open discussions with youth and providing information on these three assumptions we can begin to dismantle them. This will hopefully not only impact how they view and interact with their own body, but also how they interact with other people.

A certain weight or shape is desirable, and anything outside of that range is bad

The limited portrayal of people of different sizes, or only using people who are fat as comic relief, conveys to both kids and adults that being fat is not desirable. In surrounding kids with diversity, particularly when those who are different are appreciated and loved just the same as everyone else, it opens kids up to seeing the beauty within the differences. Thus, we are starting to unpick the assumption that only a certain weight or shape is good, and the rest are bad. By helping kids connect with each other over shared interests, actions, or characteristics of self, we are helping them move beyond appearance. Giving compliments around characteristics (such as humor or creativity) or actions, as opposed to appearance, further conveys that love and desirability does not have to be connected to appearance.

A person's weight is an indicator of their health

This assumption that underlies weight stigma is rampant. Many people who engage in weight stigma and discrimination refer to concerns about health as the rationale for their comments and actions. Some of you may have heard statements like "I am just saying this because I am concerned about your health," or "If you lost weight, this would not be an issue for you."

Sadly, there have been significant issues in the reporting of weight related research by the media and general public. Not to mention issues at the level of the research itself, which is beyond the scope and focus of this book. Research may demonstrate that something may happen more frequently in one population than another, such as a health issue in a fat population compared to a straight sized population. This is then used by the media and others as an indicator of causality, even though there may be a whole host of reasons why something may be more likely to occur in one group than another.

It is interesting to note, that a number of the issues associated with weight are also associated with prolonged exposure to discrimination, and researchers are increasingly investigating the impact of weight stigma on health.[71, 72] People who are fat experience discrimination in many areas of their life, including health care.[73] In health care symptoms are often minimized, dismissed, overlooked, or attributed to weight. As a result of this discrimination, a person may delay accessing health care due to the discomfort of weight discrimination, meanwhile their health may continue to deteriorate, and they may eventually present to health care with an even more severe condition.[74, 75] Depending on the angle of the camera, the picture you will get could be: fat people experience more severe health issues than people who are classified as average weight, or you could get: weight discrimination in health care contributes to the worsening of health issues in people who are fat. The tone and judgment from each of these pictures is very different. The message and the tone of the former drives up weight stigma and discrimination, while the latter facilitates compassion for people who are fat.

There is a growing body of literature and information that challenges the assumption that weight equates to health. Having a conversation with youth that draws attention to the complexity of weight and health helps prevent them from falling into the trap of assuming a person's health based on their weight.

A person's weight is controllable

If you look at social media, everyday conversations, and even books that were in the same store as this one, you could be led to believe that weight is easily controlled. There are many products, diets or exercise programs claiming they have the magic formula to help with weight loss, with the majority suggesting weight management is simply a matter of calories in and calories out. Eat less and move more. As a result of this messaging, when people see someone who is of a smaller build, they assume that they are small because they eat less and move more. If they see someone who is fat, they assume their size is because they eat more and move less. Applying these assumptions to ourselves and others can be hurtful, and they aren't necessarily accurate.

What else contributes to a person's weight? *A lot*. Genetics, medication, gastrointestinal health, and hormones are just a few of the many things that contribute to a person's weight.[76, 77] Two people who eat exactly the same food and do the exact same amount of exercise could have completely different responses on the scale. Weight will also naturally fluctuate over time, not just related to food and activity levels. People who weigh themselves daily may panic when they see a small increase, but that increase may be due to hormones, water, gastrointestinal health, or a myriad of other things.

When talking about the complexity of weight, and how it isn't just simply calories in/calories out, many people will draw attention to actions they have taken or someone they know have taken that was based on that formula. Will the number on the scale move if you engage in restriction and high levels of exercise? Yes, it is possible. It is not unusual to see changes on the scale when people first enter diet or exercise programs, and it fuels the illusion of controllability of weight. However, these programs are not sustainable, and the body will seek to return to the level of nutrition and weight that it needs to function optimally. What this looks like at a day-to-day level is that the longer a person is engaging in restriction or excessive activity, food craving increase, injuries occur and the number on the scale moves less. As a result, a person may stray from the diet or program by eating foods or quantities labeled as "bad" and decreasing activity. Weight is regained. Often the individual is blamed for this, and they are labelled as engaging in self sabotage, not wanting it enough or lacking will power. As the individual is seen as at fault, not the diet or program, they may then recommit to their original diet or program or go seeking another one. Weight goes up and down. Their body is put on a rollercoaster. Never knowing what to expect, it loses trust that it will consistently receive what it needs. This form of weight cycling is associated with diseases associated with obesity.[78, 79] All the while the diet and industry is making money from the growing disgust with self and body. Yet it is not the person who is to blame, it is the diet and exercise program itself.

While people strongly believe that weight is easily controllable, they will continue to jump on the weight rollercoaster, and they will judge and comment on other people's weight, as they see it as a problem that is easily fixed. By providing youth with information about the complexity of weight, and the dangers of the diet and exercise industry, we are trying to protect them from getting on the rollercoaster, and/or making assumptions of others. This is a stark contrast to the experience of many kids in the 80s and 90s, who were put on diets and brought onto the rollercoaster by loved ones.

Exposure to diversity

Many people, myself included, grew up in areas where there was a lack of significant diversity, and at the time diversity was not depicted in the media, or when it was those who were different were cast in a negative role (such as the villain, or the one who everyone laughs at). When there is a lack of diversity around us, the kids who are outside of that narrow range (whether it is weight, skin color, or ability) don't have anyone to look towards, and they can feel alone. A lack of diversity also limits comfort with, and understanding of, differences, and as a result kids can come to fear or judge the differences they notice.

If a child comes from an environment where they have witnessed judgment and discrimination against those who are different, they are more likely to engage in those behaviors in the playground. If a child hears weight comments at home about wanting to lose weight, or negative comments about self or other weight gain, or complimenting someone who has lost weight, they learn that weight loss and being thin or fit is good, and fat is bad. Thus, when they see a fat kid, they think that the child's body size is bad. Where they have been exposed to weight and body talk, they may not realize that making comments is not okay.

Out of fear of saying or doing the wrong thing, many people move to not talking at all about body, weight, or any other differences. The curious child may notice a difference and make a comment or raise a question and is then quickly hushed and told not to be rude. While this may interrupt the more overt comments or teasing, it doesn't help the child understand and accept the differences that exist. They just see a difference and think like they can't talk about it. The person is still an "other."

By surrounding children with diversity, people of all shapes, sizes, cultural backgrounds, gender expressions and abilities, we are exposing them to difference. We are putting them in the classroom where differences can be a teacher. Research on cultural diversity indicates that children who are exposed from a young age to different cultures and languages are more tolerant and open minded towards people from a different culture or who speak a different language.[78]

We can further enhance learning by having conversations. These conversations help children and teens learn that it is okay to be curious, and how their curiosity can be guided to build understanding, compassion, and empathy. To do this involves putting our own fears of doing and saying the wrong thing aside, and even being okay with saying "I don't know."

Conversations with younger children may be more focused on fostering curiosity, kindness and compassion, and decreasing judgment and hurtful acts (such as ostracizing or teasing). With children who are older or in their teens, the conversation may go deeper, exploring and challenging some of the assumptions that underpin weight stigma.

Our own actions play an important role. If we are having conversations with kids about embracing and celebrating diversity, yet then make a negative comment about people around us based on their weight or another difference, then we are giving kids mixed messages. If we are talking about celebrating diversity, and also showing it in our actions, we are giving kids a consistent message. We are talking the talk and walking the walk.

Changing the landscape takes time

One of the many things I love about hiking or walking in nature is noticing how it changes over time. There are the seasonal changes, but there is also watching trees grow over time. In trips to the Amazon forest and the Australian outback, I was amazed by the intricate weavings in these environments. What might seem like a small change could cause drastic changes in growth and survival of the plants and animals within that environment. I view the changes we engage in with ourselves and kids like changes in our natural environment. Seemingly small changes over time can lead to drastic changes in the growth and survival of body image trees, and as well as new more diverse trees. But we need to be kind and patient with ourselves and one another, as changing the landscape of the forest at a larger scale is going to take time. Furthermore, we face challenges in changing the landscape, as there are a number of industries that benefit from the landscape remaining the same, and people being trapped by the body image trees.

CHAPTER **THIRTEEN**

Change the Climate at the Industry Level

There are many industries that nurture the body image trees and are invested in maintaining the landscape of the forest. The perpetuation of weight stigma is a way to increase people's dissatisfaction with their body and increase the likelihood that they will spend money on ways to "fix" their body. A whole book could be written on this alone, but I am going to focus on four industries: diet, fashion, fitness, and social media.

Diet industry

The diet industry, of all the industries mentioned in this chapter, is one of the most toxic and stands to benefit the most from maintaining the forest landscape. The diet industry encompasses all the programs, supplements and diets targeting weight loss. It is a multibillion-dollar industry that contributes significantly to how we think and feel about our bodies. The diet industry is at the heart of diet culture, which is a system of beliefs that promote weight loss as means of achieving a state of thinness, which is worshiped and equated to moral virtue.[79] Those falling out of the ideal are often demonized and oppressed. It is important to note that in recent years terms like "diet" and "weight" are falling out of fashion, and as a result many within the industry are rebranding and repackaging as health and wellness.

It is very hard to go about your life without running into the diet industry. Everywhere you go there is talk and advertisements about the latest diet, cleanse, supplement, pill, or wellness program. The latest buzz words are used, and weight loss is connected to things you find important to lure you in. Often there is no quality research behind the product. The research used generally stops within one or two years, at which point many participants have dropped out or are starting to put the weight back on but are still below starting weight. Yet, multiple research papers exist indicating the ineffectiveness of weight loss diets and programs in the long term.[80, 81] The vast majority of people who go on diets end up putting weight back on and end up heavier than when they started.[82] This is usually omitted by the industry. What is also frequently omitted is the potential physical and mental harm associated with weight cycling. Weight cycling puts undue pressure on metabolic and cardiovascular systems, creating increased risk for health issues within these systems.[83, 84] Dieting not only doesn't lead to its intended outcome of sustained weight loss, but it harms the body.

Yet when the money has been taken, and a person starts to struggle with the diet or program (which they inevitably will because it is not sustainable for the body), rarely, if ever, is it blamed on the diet. No, instead the blame is placed on you, the person on the diet. There must be something you did wrong. You mustn't want it enough. It becomes yet another area of not being good enough. This can lead to a doubling down. A vow to try harder next time. Or it could lead to beating yourself up, and quitting.

I've had many people enter my therapy office seeking to find out why they "self sabotage" or "don't want it enough" to be able to keep "on track." Often, they are just so beat down from years of bullying from diet culture that they are completely lost and don't know what to do next. Generally, the longer a person is in the diet industry and has cycled from diet to diet, the stronger the belief that they are to blame and there is something wrong with them. What I see in my office is the impact of long-term exposure to the diet industry and diet culture, not something inherently wrong with the person.

The impact of the diet industry and diet culture extends beyond the diets and products that are being pushed, and into how we talk about food and weight. Within the diet industry there is a strong tendency to label food in a moralized manner. Food is labeled as "good" or "clean" or "bad." A label which then spreads to our actions, ourselves, and even how we view others. When talking about our actions we may say "I was good today" when we have eaten the foods deemed "good." Alternatively, when we eat things labeled "bad," we may say "I was so bad. I shouldn't have eaten that" and then experience feelings of guilt. These labels seep in, and impact how we see ourselves, particularly when there is a pattern of eating "good" or "bad." It can also impact how we view other people and their actions. They become "good" or "bad" based on what they are eating. People whose bodies may be identified as "bad" because they fall outside of the ideal, can gain the label of "good" if they are engaging in behaviors consistent with diet culture. This has led to terms like "good fatty" and "bad fatty," with the former being those who are in a larger body but expressing a desire and engaging in behaviors directed at losing weight. While the latter is a label used for those who may have rejected the pressures of the industry and diet culture, are accepting their body, and not engaging in dieting. Within all this labeling, there is a stacking of people and their worth, not based on who they are, but on how they look and whether or not they are engaging in weight loss behaviors. This is a climate that nurtures weight stigma, weight discrimination and the body image trees. Sadly, it is an industry and culture that continues to grow.

But you know what else is growing? The anti-diet movement and Health at Every Size (HAES). This movement encourages the letting go of the diet mentality, with all the "good/bad" foods and rules, and fosters moving towards making peace with food. This movement encourages rejection of the idealization and pathologizing of particular weights, and instead moving towards weight inclusivity and body acceptance. There is a growing body of literature, information online and in-person services that are anti-diet or HAES aligned. As a result there is a growing number of people learning to walk away from the diet industry, and use the time and space created from that to engage in life and connect with what is meaningful to them. An ever-growing community has formed.

What can we do?

We can starve the diet industry of money and attention, like it has starved so many people. Stepping away from and not giving money to those within the industry and their harmful empty promises. Not joining the latest program. Not buying the pills or the supplements. For many, even thinking about this can be very scary. Thoughts and fears of "What will happen when I stop? What will my body do?" These thoughts are understandable. You don't have to be alone in your journey, and you don't have to do it overnight. Explore and reach out to those connected to HAES and the anti-diet movement to gather further information and help you with those fears.

Even when people are not connected to the diet industry through being on a diet or program, they are still connected in the language they use around food. Take a moment, think about words you may attach to the following: vegetables, take-out, cookies, fruit, dairy, chicken, pasta, bread, sugar, chocolate. Did words like "good" or "bad" appear? If so, you aren't alone. Those labels can be like a spell being cast, affecting all those that touch the food. It is time to break the spell. It is food. It is not "good" or "bad," just like you are not "good" or "bad" for eating it. Again, just like stepping out of diets can be really challenging and takes time, so can lifting the moral language attached to food, food-related actions and weight. Yet there is a growing community to help support you in doing just that. As you change how you talk about food, you may also help those around you change, breaking the spell not only for you but others.

For many people caught up in the diet industry and the diet culture, their social media is full of things aimed to motivate them to lose weight. Every time you like, follow or subscribe to people and posts connected to the diet industry and diet culture, it gains power not only over you but in general. Those people producing the posts get more money, and because they are being liked they are more likely to pop up for other people. By unsubscribing and unfollowing you not only create a safe space on your own social media feed, but you also take some of the power away from those producing the posts. By finding people who embrace body diversity, HAES and anti-diet, you can fill your social media feed with content that is more accepting and encouraging of you. You are also contributing to a shift in power in the algorithms towards this content, which makes it more visible to others as well.

The diet industry and culture are huge and insidious. It is going to take a lot of time and effort to shift. There will also likely be resistance to this shift, as so much money is being made from people being unhappy with their bodies. That doesn't mean that change isn't possible, it just means we need to find each other and unite to help create change.

Fitness industry

The fitness industry and diet industry go hand in hand spreading weight stigma and diet culture and making money off people's dissatisfaction with their bodies. While the fitness industry encompasses a wide variety of groups, one of the most problematic is fitness centers or gyms. It has been found that people engaging in movement in gyms are more likely to focus on appearance and weight compared to people engaging in movement through sporting groups.[85]

I was 18 and studying at university when I first joined a gym. It was one of those big chain gyms, and it had some flashy membership deal that targeted students at the nearby university. Pending my finances and schedule I have been in and out of gyms since then. My desire to go to gyms was often convenience and wanting to move my body as my studies and my work is largely sedentary. I was worried about the impact of the sedentary lifestyle on my health, and my body. I tend to find gyms intimidating and not welcoming. When in the gym I often have felt I am being judged by others. I always found the messages plastered around many of the gyms that were meant to be motivating, aggressive and intense.

Over the years I have had numerous "assessments" with trainers when first signing up. The majority of which jumped straight to setting a goal of weight loss and seemed confused when I would state that weight loss wasn't my primary goal. Again, I would get that up and down look, but this time followed by a look that seemed to say, "Are you sure?" They would later drop into the conversation sentences like "If you did want to lose weight..." The goal of weight loss was clearly the preferred goal.

Though I have had several trainers watch my form in those "assessments" and in different classes, I can count on one hand how many actually corrected my form and provided some information on body mechanics. When I was told that one of the chain gyms hires salespeople who they then sent for a weekend fitness coaching course to then call them trainers or fitness instructors, I was not surprised.

I was in my mid-late 30s before I found a gym which had no mirrors and had trainers that were focused on form and body mechanics. There was no focus on weight loss or how my body looked. It changed my relationship with my body. I came to learn that many of the things that I thought I was doing with correct form were actually incorrect form and were making me vulnerable to pain and injury. The exact same injury and pain that I had assumed was due to me being weak, not good enough or making excuses to not push myself. In this gym I came to approach exercises and my body with curiosity. I asked which muscles I should be feeling when engaging in movement and noticed the difference in how it felt when I did correct versus incorrect form. My connection with and appreciation of my body grew. My thoughts were less focused on judgment, and more about how the body works and moves.

I had mixed feelings about this experience. On one hand I was so excited by this newfound way of connecting with my body and exercise. But on the other hand, I was angry. This is what gyms, and the fitness industry could and should be. Teaching us about our bodies, how to enjoy moving them, and how to move them correctly so we can continue to move them throughout the lifespan. Instead, we have gyms full of weight bias and weight discrimination. Multiple studies have demonstrated that exercise science students and fitness professionals have strong anti-fat bias, particularly if they have never been in a larger body.[86] Fat bodies are often used as a fear-based motivator for activities. A qualitative study[87] found that many trainers perceive weight loss as a great avenue for building confidence and feeling better about oneself, and that it can be achieved if you have the right mindset. Many would downplay the role of other factors (such as genetics, medication, metabolism) in weight, and were wary of giving those factors too much credence as they could then be used as an excuse.

It is not only the fitness professionals who hold these weight biases, people who regularly exercise at gyms have also been found to hold weight bias and believe that stigmatizing people in larger bodies will help motivate them to lose weight.[88, 89] Based on this research, if you ever walked into a gym and felt judged, your feelings were accurate. Judgment is rampant.

Yet just like there are rumblings of change and push back to the diet industry and diet culture, there are growing rumblings of change in the fitness industry. One of the core principles of Health at Every Size (HAES) is life-enhancing movement, which involves supporting "physical activities that allow people of all sizes, abilities, and interests to engage in enjoyable movement, to the degree they choose."[90] HAES seeks to assist the transition from physical activity being purely for the purpose of burning calories and changing body shape towards movement being enjoyed for the sake of physical and mental well-being. With the growing voice and presence of HAES as well as others who have grown tired of the damaging weight bias in the fitness industry, increasing pressure is being put on the industry to re-examine its intense focus on weight loss. There appears to be increased acknowledgment of the presence of weight stigma in the fitness industry and sports, as well as exploration of ways to address it and make physical activity more accessible for all bodies. In 2017, Pickett and Cunningham provided a detailed framework for creating a body inclusive space for physical activity.[91] They drew attention not only to physical changes to improve accessibility, but cultural changes to ensure people feel accepted.[92] While Ebbeck and Austin (2017)[93] have created self-compassion exercises for personal trainers which aim to increase the practice of compassion and decrease self and other judgment.

Unfortunately, at this stage there is little research on the impact of implementation of these different strategies, though Rukavina and colleagues[94] did observe a slight decrease in weight bias in kinesiology students after they participated in a multi-strategy intervention that targets weight bias.

What can we do?

As fitness centres are ultimately businesses, trying to get them to change is challenging, particularly if they perceive the change could harm their bottom dollar. Given that many personal trainers report that weight loss is the main reason a person seeks to join a gym or start training, it makes sense that this is what the industry would target and would be reluctant to let it go. Yet this does hand a little bit of control to us, the consumers. Our voices, and more importantly (from a business perspective) our money, can demonstrate that consumer needs and wants can change and are changing. We can vocalize that the use of weight focused and fat shaming advertising to lure members is not okay. That the use of insensitive "motivational" material makes people, particularly in larger bodies, feel unsafe. That the tight physical layout and machines that only handle limited shapes and sizes literally convey "you don't fit here." That we are not okay with being looked at and judged by staff and fitness professionals who make assumptions about our activity levels, our "mindset," our health and our worth purely based on our appearance. We can convey that consumer needs are changing, and if the gyms are not changing with it, then our money will go elsewhere.

And there are places we can go. There are an increasing number of body diverse inclusive spaces and HAES aligned fitness professionals emerging. Many of them are not in the big chain gyms. They may have created their own smaller studio, or they may provide individual services or services online. Moving our attention and support, especially financial, towards these and away from the weight focused gyms puts pressure on the industry to change as it is hitting the bottom dollar.

We can also use our voices to draw attention to engaging in movement for enjoyment (not weight loss), and to demonstrate that people of any size can enjoy movement. This may include interrupting people when they say things like "Oh I have to go for a long walk or run to burn that meal off," with statements like "Or you could enjoy the meal and the activity for what they are." The more we are talking or posting on social media about this, we are countering the rhetoric of movement must be about weight loss or to burn what has been eaten.

Fashion and clothing industry

The fashion and clothing industry literally sends you the message that you don't fit through clothing. If your body falls within the range of what the industry deems acceptable then you will be granted access to a wide variety of clothing in any store you walk into. You will be granted the ability to express yourself through your clothing. If your body is starting to move towards falling outside of the acceptable range, you will receive a warning that you are approaching breaching standards by it being a little harder to find your size and your selection of stores and clothing will shrink a little. Move even further away from the ideal and you will be relegated to the "plus size" section, which is usually tucked away in the back of the store, because your body being present in that store isn't good for the brand, but they still want your money. Moving even further from the ideal, you may be shoved outside of the regular stores completely, and only permitted in the plus size stores where you will be presented with an array of uninspired, very loose-fitting clothing to hide your unsightly body. If your body is beyond sizes in those stores, then you are banished to online shopping because the clothing and fashion industry doesn't want to see your body leaving the house. Through a necessary item, clothing, we are sorted and it is conveyed to us how much space we are worthy of taking up in society.

Oh, and that "standardized sizing" that we judge, beat ourselves up, and are granted permission or banished over, is based on a very narrow sampling of women taken over 40 years ago and has since been tweaked by different companies in service of vanity sizing.[95,96] In other words, the standard size is not standard and is not a reflection of the body diversity that exists in society.

It is no wonder that on any given day, there are people crying in the changerooms or avoiding going to the stores altogether. People only shopping online due to the humiliation that going into stores can bring. People wearing an article of clothing purely because it fits, not because they like it, or it reflects who they are. People walking away from the shopping experience not blaming the clothing, designers or the stores, but rather blaming themselves for not being good enough to fit what is in the store. People vowing to do what they can to fix their body so they can wear something they like. Walk into anyone's closet and chances are you will find a piece of clothing that they don't fit into now but hope to once they lose weight.

But it isn't our bodies that are the problem. It is the industry. The fashion and clothing industry is meant to design clothing to adorn bodies, not be the gatekeeper that judges what bodies are okay and not okay.[97] Yet that is what it has become. The attitudes of many of these gatekeepers towards weight are concerning and discriminatory. Many of the designers and creative directors that for years have been held up on a pedestal have expressed disdain for the larger body. A study on students of fashion design and merchandizing found that most of them held negative beliefs about weight and people in larger bodies.[98] Many of the students perceived that people are fat because of unhealthy choices in relation to diet and exercise, and a lack of willpower. If you are feeling judged by the industry, it is because you are being judged.

The teachings and tools available to those learning and entering the industry further reinforce weight stigma. The tools designers use—sketching designs, mannequins, and design programs—all are skewed towards the thin body.[99] If you are only taught about designing for thin/fit models, of course that is all you will pump out.

Yet before you throw this book across the room in a fit of rage, there is hope. Change is happening. People like Deborah Christel are introducing teaching fashion and merchandising students about weight stigma.[100] Furthermore, there is increased pressure on colleges to provide students with tools to enable them to design for diverse bodies, as indicated by students at Parsons School for Design petitioning for, and receiving, more plus size mannequins. As a result of initiatives like these, as well as of people who were tired of the limitations of mainstream clothing starting to create their own designs and lines of clothing, there is increasing availability of clothing for people of a variety of sizes.

Furthermore, there is evidence that our words and our actions can create change in this industry. It may not be as quick as we would like, but it is still movement. Even before the rise of the internet there were vocalizations and boycotts of the industry for not providing clothing beyond a particular size. In the 1980s Carole Shaw founded the *Big Beautiful Woman* magazine, which encouraged women not to feel guilty for being larger and encouraged readers to push back against the fashion industry, creating complaint slips to draw attention to perpetuation of humiliation and discrimination.[101] Initiatives like this combined with other forms of boycotting, such as letter writing, word of mouth and no longer shopping at the store or buying the product, created pressure on the industry to change and add more clothing for people who were larger. It was a step in the right direction that was made in the 80s and 90s, but clearly more steps were needed to be made as the lack of clothing for the size diverse continued to be a significant issue.

With the internet, and particularly social media, it is easier than ever to have a voice and form a community of people with the shared interest of social justice. This collective voice has increasingly been putting pressure on designer brands and clothing stores to listen to the consumer and respond to the diversity that exists. The 2018 #MakeMySize movement, initiated by Katie Sturino, is an example of how social media can be used to create pressure on brands to diversify their output. Under this movement, people would post about clothing that they liked that was not in their size asking the manufacturer to make it in a larger size. This resulted in several brands adding to their size range.[102]

The internet and social media also allow us to see people of all shapes, sizes, race, and gender identification, find clothing that they can feel comfortable and express themselves in. This creates hope that people no longer have to just settle for what is available in their size. Online you can find and access nonmainstream clothing providers, who are more attuned to meeting the needs of diverse bodies. Every time someone goes to these online providers, they are taking money away from the mainstream fashion gatekeepers and putting it in the hands of the community.

What can we do?

So, what can we learn from this? At the level of the industry itself, there needs to be increased weight stigma education, and resources available to teach people how to make clothes for a variety of body shapes and sizes. Clothing stores need to provide greater selection of sizes and have them integrated together, not shoving people beyond a certain size to another part of the store or another store altogether. While we are talking about store layout, making the layout and changerooms more accessible would also be helpful. Bonus points for stores that provide their staff with training on weight stigma so that they are not engaging in behaviors (such as that up and down look) which are denigrating to those entering the store.

At the level of consumers, there is a lot we can do. We don't have to settle for mediocrity of clothing and options. In a capitalist world, money speaks volumes and through our voices and actions we can change where the money flows. We can unite online and have a voice. A voice that calls out stores and brands that perpetuate weight stigma by only carrying a very narrow range of sizes. A voice that celebrates stores and brands that do support diversity. I mean real diversity, not just having models or mannequins that are one or maybe two sizes above the norm (the plus size that isn't really a plus size), or the token image or model that is not white. Celebrate the stores and brands that actually make clothing for people of a variety of shapes and sizes, and genuinely embrace diversity. We can have a voice that helps people believe they can express themselves with their clothing, and don't have to follow rules of what they can and can't wear because of the shape and size of their body.

Social media industry

I left this industry till last, not because I don't think it has an important influence on the climate and struggles in the forest, but because I find many people use social media as a way of over-simplifying and invalidating struggles with body and weight. It is similar to previous years when people would point the finger at magazines and media as being to blame for the rise in weight stigma, body image issues and eating disorders. It implies that the struggle is just about appearance. As stated throughout this book, the struggles are not just about appearance. Struggles with weight and body image are about fighting to be seen, heard, have worth, and belong. Social media is a piece of the puzzle, but it is not the only piece.

The combination of our social media feeds consisting of people who are peers (as opposed to celebrities of movies and television) and the sheer mass of posting, increases perception of normalcy and accessibility of the thin/fit ideal. This can then drive up the internal dialogue of our bodies not being good enough, and a problem that needs to be fixed.

Yet, as indicated by some of what has already been noted in this chapter, social media doesn't have to be a source of unhelpful and unhealthy messages. Social media can be used to connect people who are like minded, allow them to start movements and to be seen, heard, and matter.

What can we do?

Creating change in social media can be broken down into steps. The first two are about reducing the influence and challenging unhelpful and harmful content, while the remaining steps are about creating a space that is helpful, supportive and ignites you.

Step one: Take the numbers away

Unfollow, unsubscribe, unlike anything that perpetuates weight stigma, diet culture, weight-focused movement, lack of diverse fashion, and anything else that makes you feel bad about your body. In the online world, numbers matter. The more likes, follows, and subscribes something gets, the more it will be pushed. By unfollowing, unsubscribing, and unliking, and encouraging others to do the same, you are taking those numbers away from those sources and reducing their influence. Yes, the person or company will continue to post, but their influence and impact will shrink.

Step two: Challenge the message

If you do see things that are unhelpful or harmful, speak up. You can report the content to the platform that you are on and seek to have it removed. You could provide information that challenges the post and suggest an alternative. You can message the person or organization, seeking clarification, understanding, and sharing of information. When speaking up, I encourage you to do so calmly, compassionately, and with solid information. No one responds well when being yelled at, called names or other negative impressions implied. When that occurs defenses go up, and whatever messages were trying to be conveyed get lost.

Step three: Move the numbers to somewhere helpful

Follow, subscribe, and like things that promote body diversity and acceptance, as well as that which helps you connect with things beyond your body (remember you are more than your body). Your social media feed doesn't need to be something that leaves you riddled with anxiety, sadness, guilt, and shame. It can be something that inspires you, and helps you connect with others.

Step four: Connect with the community

Connect with people in the community. If they post things you really enjoy or find helpful, let them know. Many of those who are creating content that embraces body diversity get pushback. It can be helpful for them to know that there are people who find their content meaningful. In reaching out, you are also building your sense of belonging and connection. These connections and sense of belonging may be particularly helpful when you encounter struggles along your journey. These are the people you can turn to when you need help to keep going when you encounter pushback or hit a wall.

Step five: Add to the content

Many of us have hidden in the shadows throughout our lives. Not having a voice. Not wanting to be seen. Thinking that we have nothing to bring or that we don't matter. *But* we do matter! We have thoughts, feelings, ideas, and things to say that matter. We can make a difference not only for ourselves but for those around us. Don't wait. Step into the spotlight. Be seen. You matter.

A call to action

When I look at all the things that contribute to the climate that nurtures the body image trees, I can get overwhelmed. Throughout writing this book I was scared, as often my attention would be drawn to those who are maintaining the current landscape, nurturing the body image trees. The ones I suspect will push back, as I see them push back whenever someone puts forward something showing someone in a larger body with angry cries of "You are glorifying obesity." I have used many of the tools I have written about in this book to help me write this book.

When I think of my own experiences, the experiences of the people close to me, the experiences of my clients, and the experiences of all those I haven't met who are being oppressed and having their life stifled because of the climate we live in and how it regards body and weight. I can hold that fear of the pushback, and I can keep going because all those people matter. We all deserve to be living the life we want to live. We all should be able to unapologetically take up space in the world. We all deserve to belong. We all deserve to not have to put our lives on hold and wait until we look a certain way to be accepted in society.

What I think is really cool is that we can join together and create spaces that convey exactly that. So, I am making a call to action. Let us create spaces and communities where people can feel safe to be seen. Let us teach and raise children in those spaces and protect them from facing the societal messages we faced. Let us join those spaces and communities together, making them spread so that safety and celebration of diversity is shared and begins to become the norm. Let us create a world where we can dance through the forest taking in all the different sights and experiences. Let us create a world where we, nor anyone else, feel they have to change their body in order to live the life they want to live.

Endnotes

1 Porges, S. W. (2021). Polyvagal theory: A biobehavioral journey to sociality. *Comprehensive Psychoneuroendocrinology*, 7.

2 Porges, S. W. (1995). Orienting in a defensive world: Mammalian modifications of our evolutionary heritage. A polyvagal theory. *Psychophysiology*, *32*(4), 301–318.

3 Porges, S. W. (2001). The polyvagal theory: phylogenetic substrates of a social nervous system. *International Journal of Psychophysiology*, *42*(2), 123–146.

4 Porges, S. W. (2003). Social engagement and attachment: a phylogenetic perspective. *Annals of the New York Academy of Sciences*, *1008*(1), 31–47.

5 Eisenberger, N. I., Lieberman, M. D., and Williams, K. D. (2003). Does rejection hurt? An fMRI study of social exclusion. *Science*, *302*(5643), 290–292.

6 Williams, K. D. (2009). Ostracism: A Temporal Need-Threat Model. In M. Zanna (Ed.), *Advances in Experimental Social Psychology*. New York: Academic Press.

7 Törneke, N. (2010). *Learning RFT: An Introduction to Relational Frame Theory and Its Clinical Application*. Oakland, CA: Context Press/New Harbinger Publications.

8 Brun, I., Russell-Mayhew, S., and Mudry, T. (2021). Last word: Ending the intergenerational transmission of body dissatisfaction and disordered eating: A call to investigate the mother–daughter relationship. *Eating Disorders*, *29*(6), 591–598.

9 Gillen, M. M., and Lefkowitz, E. S. (2009). Emerging adults' perceptions of messages about physical appearance. *Body Image*, *6*(3), 178–185.

10 Brun, I., Russell-Mayhew, S., and Mudry, T. (2021). Last Word: Ending the intergenerational transmission of body dissatisfaction and disordered eating: a call to investigate the mother-daughter relationship. *Eating Disorders*, *29*(6), 591-598.

11 Smolak, L., Levine, M. P., and Schermer, F. (1999). Parental input and weight concerns among elementary school children. *International Journal of Eating Disorders*, *25*(3), 263–271.

12 Keery, H., Boutelle, K., Van Den Berg, P., and Thompson, J. K. (2005). The impact of appearance-related teasing by family members. *Journal of Adolescent Health*, *37*(2), 120–127.

13 Schaefer, M. K., and Salafia, E. H. B. (2014). The connection of teasing by parents, siblings, and peers with girls' body dissatisfaction and boys' drive for muscularity: The role of social comparison as a mediator. *Eating Behaviors*, *15*(4), 599–608.

14 Thomas, S. L., Olds, T., Pettigrew, S., Randle, M., and Lewis, S. (2014). "Don't eat that, you'll get fat!" Exploring how parents and children conceptualise and frame messages about the causes and consequences of obesity. *Social Science and Medicine*, *119*, 114–122.

15 Kluck, A. S. (2010). Family influence on disordered eating: The role of body image dissatisfaction. *Body Image*, *7*(1), 8–14.

16 Oliveira, S., Marta-Simões, J., and Ferreira, C. (2019). Early parental eating messages and disordered eating: The role of body shame and inflexible eating. *The Journal of Psychology*, *153*(6), 615–627.

17 Oliveira, S., Pires, C., and Ferreira, C. (2020). Does the recall of caregiver eating messages exacerbate the pathogenic impact of shame on eating and weight-related difficulties? *Eating and Weight Disorders-Studies on Anorexia, Bulimia and Obesity*, *25*(2), 471–480.

18 Rodgers, R. F., Paxton, S. J., and Chabrol, H. (2009). Effects of parental comments on body dissatisfaction and eating disturbance in young adults: A sociocultural model. *Body Image*, *6*(3), 171–177.

19 Puhl, R. M., Wall, M. M., Chen, C., Austin, S. B., Eisenberg, M. E., and Neumark-Sztainer, D. (2017). Experiences of weight teasing in adolescence and weight-related outcomes in adulthood: A 15-year longitudinal study. *Preventive Medicine*, *100*, 173–179.

20 Harriger, J. A., Serier, K. N., Luedke, M., Robertson, S., and Bojorquez, A. (2018). Appearance-related themes in children's animated movies released between 2004 and 2016: A content analysis. *Body Image*, *26*, 78–82.

21 Klein, H., and Shiffman, K. S. (2005). Thin is "in" and stout is "out": What animated cartoons tell viewers about body weight. *Eating and Weight Disorders-Studies on Anorexia, Bulimia and Obesity*, *10*(2), 107–116.

22 Klein, H., and Shiffman, K. S. (2006). Messages about physical attractiveness in animated cartoons. *Body Image*, *3*(4), 353–363.

23 Tzoutzou, M., Bathrellou, E., and Matalas, A. L. (2021). Cartoon characters in children's series: Gender disparities in body weight and food consumption. *Sexes*, *2*(1), 79–87.

24 Ata, R. N., and Thompson, J. K. (2010). Weight bias in the media: A review of recent research. *Obesity Facts, 3*(1), 41–46.

25 Greenberg, B. S., Eastin, M., Hofschire, L., Lachlan, K., and Brownell, K. D. (2003). Portrayals of overweight and obese individuals on commercial television. *American Journal of Public Health, 93*(8), 1342–1348.

26 Cameron, L. (2019). The "good fatty" is a dancing fatty: Fat archetypes in reality television. *Fat Studies,* 8(3), 259–278.

27 Roost, A. (2016). Losing it: The construction and stigmatization of obesity on reality television in the United States. *The Journal of Popular Culture* 49(1), 174–195.

28 Cramer, P., and Steinwert, T. (1998). Thin is good, fat is bad: How early does it begin?. *Journal of Applied Developmental Psychology, 19*(3), 429–451.

29 Thompson, I., Hong, J. S., Lee, J. M., Prys, N. A., Morgan, J. T., and Udo-Inyang, I. (2020). A review of the empirical research on weight-based bullying and peer victimisation published between 2006 and 2016. *Educational Review, 72*(1), 88–110.

30 Puhl, R. M., and King, K. M. (2013). Weight discrimination and bullying. *Best Practice and Research Clinical Endocrinology and Metabolism, 27*(2), 117–127.

31 Browne, N. T. (2012). Weight bias, stigmatization, and bullying of obese youth. *Bariatric Nursing and Surgical Patient Care,* 7(3), 107–115.

32 Puhl, R. M., Latner, J. D., O'brien, K., Luedicke, J., Forhan, M., and Danielsdottir, S. (2016). Cross-national perspectives about weight-based bullying in youth: nature, extent and remedies. *Pediatric Obesity, 11*(4), 241–250.

33 Puhl, R. M., Luedicke, J., and Heuer, C. (2011). Weight-based victimization toward overweight adolescents: observations and reactions of peers. *Journal of School Health, 81*(11), 696–703.

34 Nichter, M. (2002). *Fat talk: What girls and their parents say about dieting.* Cambridge: Harvard University Press.

35 Salk, R. H., and Engeln-Maddox, R. (2011). "If you're fat, then I'm humongous!" Frequency, content, and impact of fat talk among college women. *Psychology of Women Quarterly, 35*(1), 18–28.

36 Cruwys, T., Leverington, C. T., and Sheldon, A. M. (2016). An experimental investigation of the consequences and social functions of fat talk in friendship groups. *International Journal of Eating Disorders, 49*(1), 84–91.

37 Engeln, R., and Salk, R. H. (2016). The demographics of fat talk in adult women: Age, body size, and ethnicity. *Journal of Health Psychology, 21*(8), 1655–1664.

38 Shannon, A., and Mills, J. S. (2015). Correlates, causes, and consequences of fat talk: A review. *Body Image, 15,* 158–172.

39 Shannon, A., and Mills, J. S. (2015). Correlates, causes, and consequences of fat talk: A review. *Body Image, 15*, 158–172.

40 Britton, L. E., Martz, D. M., Bazzini, D. G., Curtin, L. A., and LeaShomb, A. (2006). Fat talk and self-presentation of body image: Is there a social norm for women to self-degrade? *Body Image, 3*(3), 247–254.

41 Salk, R. H., and Engeln-Maddox, R. (2011). "If you're fat, then I'm humongous!" Frequency, content, and impact of fat talk among college women. *Psychology of Women Quarterly, 35*(1), 18–28.

42 Becker, C. B., Diedrichs, P. C., Jankowski, G., and Werchan, C. (2013). I'm not just fat, I'm old: has the study of body image overlooked "old talk"? *Journal of Eating Disorders, 1*(1), 1–12.

43 Chou, W. Y. S., Prestin, A., and Kunath, S. (2014). Obesity in social media: A mixed methods analysis. *Translational Behavioral Medicine, 4*(3), 314–323.

44 Lupton, D. (2017). Digital media and body weight, shape, and size: An introduction and review. *Fat Studies, 6*(2), 119–134.

45 Yoo, J. H., and Kim, J. (2012). Obesity in the new media: A content analysis of obesity videos on YouTube. *Health Communication, 27*(1), 86–97.

46 Ghaznavi, J., and Taylor, L. D. (2015). Bones, body parts, and sex appeal: An analysis of #thinspiration images on popular social media. *Body Image, 14*, 54–61.

47 Tiggemann, M., and Zaccardo, M. (2018). "Strong is the new skinny": A content analysis of #fitspiration images on Instagram. *Journal of Health Psychology, 23*(8), 1003–1011.

48 Boepple, L., and Thompson, J. K. (2016). A content analytic comparison of fitspiration and thinspiration websites. *International Journal of Eating Disorders, 49*(1), 98–101.

49 Talbot, C. V., Gavin, J., Van Steen, T., and Morey, Y. (2017). A content analysis of thinspiration, fitspiration, and bonespiration imagery on social media. *Journal of Eating Disorders, 5*(1), 1–8.

50 Cohen, R., Irwin, L., Newton-John, T., and Slater, A. (2019). #bodypositivity: A content analysis of body positive accounts on Instagram. *Body Image, 29*, 47–57.

51 Tylka, T. L., and Wood-Barcalow, N. L. (2015). What is and what is not positive body image? Conceptual foundations and construct definition. *Body Image, 14*, 118–129.

52 Cohen, R., Newton-John, T., and Slater, A. (2021). The case for body positivity on social media: Perspectives on current advances and future directions. *Journal of Health Psychology, 26*(13), 2365–2373.

53 Muttarak, R. (2018). Normalization of plus size and the danger of unseen overweight and obesity in England. *Obesity, 26*(7), 1125–1129.

54 Alleva, J. M., and Tylka, T. L. (2018). Muttarak's study design cannot support the link between the body-positive movement and overweight or obesity. *Obesity*, *26*(10), 1527–1529.

55 Côté, M., and Bégin, C. (2020). Review of the experience of weight-based stigmatization in romantic relationships. *Current Obesity Reports*, *9*(3), 280–287.

56 Cawley, J., Joyner, K., and Sobal, J. (2006). Size matters: The influence of adolescents' weight and height on dating and sex. *Rationality and Society*, *18*(1), 67–94.

57 Carriere, L. J., and Kluck, A. S. (2014). Appearance commentary from romantic partners: Evaluation of an adapted measure. *Body Image*, *11*(2), 137–145.

58 Collisson, B., Howell, J. L., Rusbasan, D., and Rosenfeld, E. (2017). "Date someone your own size": Prejudice and discrimination toward mixed-weight relationships. *Journal of Social and Personal Relationships*, *34*(4), 510–540.

59 Puhl, R. M., and Heuer, C. A. (2009). The stigma of obesity: A review and update. *Obesity*, *17*(5), 941.

60 Rudolph, C. W., Wells, C. L., Weller, M. D., and Baltes, B. B. (2009). A meta-analysis of empirical studies of weight-based bias in the workplace. *Journal of Vocational Behavior*, *74*(1), 1–10.

61 Puhl, R., and Brownell, K. D. (2002). Stigma, discrimination, and obesity. *Eating Disorders and Obesity: A Comprehensive Handbook*, 2, 108–112.

62 Puhl, R. M., and Heuer, C. A. (2009). The stigma of obesity: A review and update. *Obesity*, *17*(5), 941.

63 Hayes, S. C., and Strosahl, K. D. (Eds). (2004). *A Practical Guide to Acceptance and Commitment Therapy*. New York: Springer-Verlag.

64 Wilson, K. G., Sandoz, E. K., Kitchens, J., and Roberts, M. (2010). The Valued Living Questionnaire: Defining and measuring valued action within a behavioral framework. *The Psychological Record*, *60*(2), 249–272.

65 Tseng, J., and Poppenk, J. (2020). Brain meta-state transitions demarcate thoughts across task contexts exposing the mental noise of trait neuroticism. *Nature Communications*, *11*(1), 1–12.

66 Brown, B. (2017). *Braving the Wilderness: The Quest for True Belonging and the Courage to Stand Alone*. New York: Random House.

67 Brown, B. (2017). *Braving the Wilderness: The Quest for True Belonging and the Courage to Stand Alone*. New York: Random House, p.41.

68 Brown, B. (2017). *Braving the Wilderness: The Quest for True Belonging and the Courage to Stand Alone*. New York: Random House.

69 Dores Cruz, T. D., Nieper, A. S., Testori, M., Martinescu, E., and Beersma, B. (2021). An integrative definition and framework to study gossip. *Group and Organization Management*, *46*(2), 252–285.

70 Grosser, T., Kidwell, V., and Labianca, G. J. (2012). Hearing it through the grapevine: Positive and negative workplace gossip. *Organizational Dynamics*, *41*, 52–61.

71 Daly, M., Sutin, A. R., and Robinson, E. (2019). Perceived weight discrimination mediates the prospective association between obesity and physiological dysregulation: Evidence from a population-based cohort. *Psychological Science*, *30*(7), 1030–1039.

72 Sutin, A. R., Stephan, Y., and Terracciano, A. (2015). Weight discrimination and risk of mortality. *Psychological Science*, *26*, 1803–1811.

73 Puhl, R. M., and Brownell, K. D. (2006). Confronting and coping with weight stigma: An investigation of overweight and obese adults. *Obesity*, *14*(10), 1802–1815.

74 Kasten, G. (2018). Listen... and speak: A discussion of weight bias, its intersections with homophobia, racism, and misogyny, and their impacts on health. *Canadian Journal of Dietetic Practice and Research*, *79*(3), 133–138.

75 Tomiyama, A. J., Carr, D., Granberg, E. M., Major, B., Robinson, E., Sutin, A. R., and Brewis, A. (2018). How and why weight stigma drives the obesity "epidemic" and harms health. *BMC Medicine*, *16*(1), 1–6.

76 Daníelsdóttir, S., O'Brien, K. S., and Ciao, A. (2010). Anti-fat prejudice reduction: A review of published studies. *Obesity Facts*, *3*(1), 47–58.

77 Kyle, T. K., Dhurandhar, E. J., and Allison, D. B. (2016). Regarding obesity as a disease: Evolving policies and their implications. *Endocrinology and Metabolism Clinics*, *45*(3), 511–520.

78 Aboud, F. E., Tredoux, C., Tropp, L. R., Brown, C. S., Niens, U., and Noor, N. M. (2012). Interventions to reduce prejudice and enhance inclusion and respect for ethnic differences in early childhood: A systematic review. *Developmental Review*, *32*(4), 307–336.

79 Harrison, C., and Harrison, C. (2019). *Anti-diet*. Boston, MA: Little, Brown.

80 Aaseth, J., Ellefsen, S., Alehagen, U., Sundfør, T. M., and Alexander, J. (2021). Diets and drugs for weight loss and health in obesity—An update. *Biomedicine and Pharmacotherapy*, *140*, 111789.

81 Tomiyama, A. J., Ahlstrom, B., and Mann, T. (2013). Long-term effects of dieting: Is weight loss related to health?. *Social and Personality Psychology Compass*, *7*(12), 861–877.

82 Adams, L., and Willer, F. (2017). *Everything You Have Been Told About Weightloss is Bullshit*. Ebook.

83 Montani, J. P., Viecelli, A. K., Prévot, A., and Dulloo, A. G. (2006). Weight cycling during growth and beyond as a risk factor for later cardiovascular

diseases: The "repeated overshoot" theory. *International Journal of Obesity*, *30*(4), S58–S66.

84 Montani, J. P., Schutz, Y., and Dulloo, A. G. (2015). Dieting and weight cycling as risk factors for cardiometabolic diseases: Who is really at risk? *Obesity Reviews*, *16*, 7–18.

85 Kilpatrick, M., Hebert, E., and Bartholomew, J. (2005). College students' motivation for physical activity: Differentiating men's and women's motives for sport participation and exercise. *Journal of American College Health*, *54*(2), 87–94.

86 Panza, G. A., Armstrong, L. E., Taylor, B. A., Puhl, R. M., Livingston, J., and Pescatello, L. S. (2018). Weight bias among exercise and nutrition professionals: A systematic review. *Obesity Reviews*, *19*(11), 1492–1503.

87 Donaghue, N., and Allen, M. (2016). "People don't care as much about their health as they do about their looks": Personal trainers as intermediaries between aesthetic and health-based discourses of exercise participation and weight management. *International Journal of Sport and Exercise Psychology*, *14*(1), 42–56.

88 Flint, S. W., and Reale, S. (2018). Weight stigma in frequent exercisers: Overt, demeaning and condescending. *Journal of Health Psychology*, *23*(5), 710–719.

89 Robertson, N., and Vohora, R. (2008). Fitness vs. fatness: Implicit bias towards obesity among fitness professionals and regular exercisers. *Psychology of Sport and Exercise*, *9*(4), 547–557.

90 Association for Size Diversity and Health. (2014). Health at Every Size (HAES) Principles. Accessed at http://asdah.org/health-at-every-size-haes-approach on 02/21/23.

91 Pickett, A. C., and Cunningham, G. B. (2017). Physical activity for every-body: A model for managing weight stigma and creating body-inclusive spaces. *Quest*, *69*(1), 19–36.

92 Cunningham, G. B., and Pickett, A. C. (2020). The importance of perceived body-inclusiveness among physically active women in larger bodies. *Sex Roles*, *83*(11), 754–762.

93 Ebbeck, V., and Austin, S. (2018). Burning off the fat oppression: Self-compassion exercises for personal trainers. *Fat Studies*, *7*(1), 81–92.

94 Rukavina, P. B., Li, W., Shen, B., and Sun, H. (2010). A service learning based project to change implicit and explicit bias toward obese individuals in kinesiology pre-professionals. *Obesity Facts*, *3*(2), 117–126.

95 Bishop, K., Gruys, K., and Evans, M. (2018). Sized out: Women, clothing size, and inequality. *Gender and Society*, *32*(2), 180–203.

96 Hackett, L. J., and Rall, D. N. (2018). The size of the problem with the problem of sizing: How clothing measurement systems have misrepresented women's bodies, from the 1920s to today. *Clothing Cultures*, 5(2), 263–283.
97 Christel, D. A. (2014). It's your fault you're fat: Judgements of responsibility and social conduct in the fashion industry. *Clothing Cultures*, 1(3), 303–320.
98 Christel, D. A. (2014). It's your fault you're fat: Judgements of responsibility and social conduct in the fashion industry. *Clothing Cultures*, 1(3), 303–320.
99 Christel, D. A. (2017). Fat fashion: Fattening pedagogy in apparel design. *Fat Studies*, 7(1), 44–55.
100 Christel, D. A. (2016). Obesity education as an intervention to reduce weight bias in fashion students. *Journal of Education and Learning*, 5(2), 170–179.
101 Peters, L. D. (2021). Discourses of discontent: fashion, feminism and the commodification of fat women's anger. *Fat Studies*, 11(1), 1–14.
102 Peters, L. D. (2021). Discourses of discontent: fashion, feminism and the commodification of fat women's anger. *Fat Studies*, 11(1), 1–14.

Subject Index

Sub-headings in *italics* indicate tables.

abuse 65
acceptance 87–8, 89
  choose your own adventure 89–90
  mapping out your pool 90–1
acknowledgement exercise 86–7
ACT (Acceptance and Commitment Therapy) 18–20, 38, 94
admiration 50–1
  who do I admire? 51–2
aerial arts 99–100, 137–9
anger 66, 84–5, 87, 106, 108, 110
anxiety 20, 32, 50, 97, 104, 105, 111, 114, 118
  social media 187
  WIIFI (what if I f**ck it up?) 115
appearance 16–17
assumptions underlying weight stigma 168
  only a certain weight or shape is desirable 168–9
  weight is an indicator of health 169
  weight is controllable 170–2
avoidance 81–5
awareness 74
  awareness of past hurt 151–3

behavior change 20
belonging 125, 134
  being seen 128–31
  belonging from the inside 126–7
  fitting in versus belonging 125–6
  small steps to being seen and creating connection 131–4
  who am I? 127–8
  you belong as you are 167–8
Big Beautiful Women 184
blaming 67, 149, 183
body image 15–20, 21, 65
  being human 21–3, 32–3
  body and values 53–4
  exploring memories 67–71
  Influence of messages around body and weight 73
  influences on body image 23–31
  put on your glasses of compassion and curiosity 65–7
  weight bias, stigma and discrimination 31–2
  see also dealing with body image
  see taking new steps
brain function 21–3, 66
breathing 112
  box breathing 112
  slowing the breath 112–13
Brown, Brené Braving the Wilderness 128
bullying 16, 26–7, 160, 176

change 74
keep going 142–4
past barriers to sustaining change 143
tackling future barriers 143
taking action 140–2, 144
changing the dialogues 147
changing the dialogue at different levels 153–61
Choose your own adventure 156
interrupting unhelpful acts 149–53
micro acts of kindness 147–9
ripples in a pond 161–2
your actions towards others 156–8
your response to other people's actions 159–61
your thoughts and judgments towards others 154–5
changing the story 117, 122–3
troubleshooting some common traps 120–2
typecasting 118–20
write your story 122
your characters 118, 122
Christel, Deborah 184
circus arts 99–100, 137–9
climate (of weight stigma) 23–31, 32–3, 188
weight bias, stigma and discrimination 31–2
working together to change the climate 168–73
clothing 61–2, 82
clothes shopping 147–9
fashion and clothing industry 182–5
compassion 43, 45, 47, 51, 114
put on your glasses of compassion and curiosity 65–7, 138–9
connecting with others
find your voice 132–3
look up 131–2
notice your environment 133–4
connecting with yourself 60–2
no need to wait 62–4
take action to connect with what is important 111
conversation 132–3, 172–3
courage 43, 51, 61
curiosity 67
put on your glasses of compassion and curiosity 65–7, 138–9
dating 30, 130, 141
dealing with body image 77–8
acceptance 87–91
acknowledgement exercise 86–7
avoid it 81–5
common responses 78–9
fix it or problem-solve 79–81
letting go of struggle 85–6
self-reflection exercise 84–5
see also body image
defusion 93
fusion versus defusion 97–100
troubleshooting defusion 97–9
we think a lot 93–5
depression 20, 32, 83, 97
diet industry 175–7
what can we do? 177–8
direction 37–9, 55
body and values 53–4
time machine exercises 39–50
values as compass 38–9
values lists and cards 54–5
who do I admire? 50–2
discrimination 31–2
disordered eating 25, 71
distraction activities 83–4
diversity 171–3
domains of your life 38–9, 47, 59–60, 69

eating disorders 32, 65, 69, 149, 186
emotions 50, 65, 101–2, 116
  anger 108, 110
  exploring messages you received about emotions 102–3
  fear 107, 109–10
  guilt 107–8, 110, 111
  happiness 109, 110
  I feel because I care 106–9
  love 109, 110
  Messages about emotions 102
  negative memories 43–5
  noticing 105–6
  sadness 107, 110
  self-reflection questions 103, 105–6, 109–10
  shame 107–8, 110
  take action to connect with what is important 111
  tools to keep moving in the face of the emotion 112–14
  what am I feeling? 103–4
  your own signposts? 114–16
exclusion 26–7, 148

family environment 23–5, 68–9
fashion and clothing industry 182–5
  what can we do? 185
fatness 15, 24, 31, 32, 68–72, 150, 180, 183
  assumptions underlying weight stigma 168–71
  children 26–7
  employment 31
  "fat talk" 27–8, 149
  Influence of messages around body and weight 73
  sex 30
  social media 28–9, 81
fear 69–70, 87, 98, 104, 106, 107, 109–10, 159–60
fitness industry 179–81
  what can we do? 181–2
fitting in versus belonging 125–6
fixing it approaches 79–81
forest (of weight stigma) 15–20, 21, 65, 93, 135–6, 147, 175, 188
  acceptance of the forest 89–91
  avoidance of the painful body image trees 78–85
  awareness creates space for change 74
  changing the landscape takes time 173
  continuing in the forest 91
  forest visualization 95–6
  helping kids navigate the forest 163–8
  Influence of messages around body and weight 73
  navigating your forest 37–9, 57–9
  put on your glasses of compassion and curiosity 65–7
  story of you in the forest 122–3
  time for bigger change in the forest 144
  time machine to explore the beginning of your forest 67–74
future 39–40
  future-negative 48
  future-negative exercise 49
  future-negative troubleshooting 50
  future-positive 46
  future-positive 46–7
  future-positive troubleshooting 47–8
  tackling future barriers 143

Gandhi, Mahatma 163
goal setting 140–1
gossip 133

guided exercises
acknowledge 86–7
noticing 105
ripple visualization 162
guilt 66, 68, 69, 80, 84–5, 98, 104, 106, 107, 110, 150

happiness 39, 106, 109, 110
Hayes, Steven 38, 94
Health at Every Size (HAES) 177–8, 180–2

ideal body–not-ideal body 53–4
improv classes 136
industries 80, 175
diet industry 175–8
fashion and clothing industry 182–5
fitness industry 179–82
social media industry 186–8

kindness 43, 45, 47, 51
interrupting unhelpful acts 149–53
micro acts of kindness 147–9

language 22–3
laughter 16
love 17, 29, 106, 109
low self-esteem 25, 32

#MakeMySize 184
mapping out your pool exercise 90–1
memories 39–40, 65
be the person you needed 163–6
exploring memories 67–71
past-negative 43–5
past-positive 40–3
motivation 57–9
connect with you 60–2
prioritizing your values 59–60
recharging your motivation 64
what makes a good...? 62–4
music 61, 113, 123

obesity 30, 32, 171, 188
ostracizing 16, 22, 173

past 39–40
awareness of past hurt 151–3
past barriers to sustaining change 143
past-negative 43
past-negative exercise 44
past-negative troubleshooting 45
past-positive 40–1
past-positive exercise 41–2
past-positive troubleshooting 42–3
peer interactions 26–8
posture 61
problem-solving approaches 79–81

roller derby 61

sadness 43–5, 66, 82, 104, 106, 107, 110, 111
self-judgement 16
self-reflection exercises
awareness of past hurt 152–3
be the person you needed 165–6
changing actions towards others 158
changing response to other people's actions 160–1
soothing senses 113–14
what path do I take? 84
self-reflection moments
awareness of past hurt 151–2
different world 128
fit in or belong 126
have you typecast yourself? 119
past barriers to sustaining change 143
small steps to values 142
tackling future barriers 143
what prevents you from being seen? 130
your characters 118

self-reflection questions
a nod to emotions 105–6
how my forest shaped me 74
my emotion messages 103
what are my emotions telling me? 109–10
sex 30, 82
shame 29–30, 66, 68, 69, 80, 84–5, 98, 104, 106, 107–8, 110, 150
shaming 28–9, 67, 149, 181
Shaw, Carole 184
signposts to emotion 114
create your signpost 115–16
WIIFI (what if I f••ck it up?) 115
smell 61–2
social climate 23–31
working together to change the climate 168–73
social engagement 21
avoidance 81–5
being seen 128–31
being seen and creating connection 131–4
brain function 21–2, 66
language 22–3
social media 28–30, 186
what can we do? 186–8
soothing 113–14
stigma 31–2, 168–71
struggling 85–6
Sturino, Katie 184

tactile sensations 61–2, 113
taking new steps (some things to remember) 135–6
don't believe the highlights reel is the norm 139
keep those compassion and curiosity glasses at hand 138–9
you don't have to do it on your own 139–40
you will make mistakes and fail 136–7
you will suck 137–8
teasing 16, 24–5, 26, 28–9, 30, 69–71, 172–3
television 25–6
thoughts 93–4
thought experiment 1: I'm having a thought 94–5
thought experiment 2: Forest visualization 95–6
thought experiment 3: My conditioning 96
thought experiment 4: Workability 96
time machine 39–40
future-negative 48–9
future-negative troubleshooting 50
future-positive 46–7
future-positive troubleshooting 47–8
past-negative 43–4
past-negative troubleshooting 45
past-positive 40–2
past-positive troubleshooting 42–3
trauma 43, 65
typecasting 118–19
breaking the typecast 119–20
troubleshooting some common traps 120–2

values 38–9, 55, 69–70
admiration 50–1
body and values 53–4
connect with you 60–2
prioritizing your values 59–60
small steps to values 142
values lists and cards 54–5
what makes a good...? 62–4
who do I admire? 51–2
see time machine

website links 41, 43, 46, 48, 60, 72, 102, 104, 127, 162
weight 15
  avoidance responses 81–5
  exposure to diversity 171–3
  fitting in versus belonging 125–6
  fix it or problem-solve approaches 79–81
  Influence of messages around body and weight 73
  no need to wait 62–4
  put on your glasses of compassion and curiosity 65–7
  unpicking the assumptions underlying weight stigma 168–71
weight bias, stigma and discrimination 31–2
workplace 31, 159–60

young people 163
  be the person you needed 163–6
  changing the landscape takes time 173
  helping kids navigate the forest 163–8
  sit with them through the pain 166
  working together to change the climate 168–73
  you belong as you are 167–8

Author Index

Aaseth, J. 176
Aboud, F. E. 171, 172
Adams, L. 176
Ahlstrom, B. 176
Alehagen, U. 176
Alexander, J. 176
Allen, M. 180
Alleva, J. M. 30
Allison, D. B. 170
Armstrong, L. E. 180
Association for Size Diversity and Health 180
Ata, R. N. 25
Austin, S. 25, 181

Baltes, B. B. 31
Bartholomew, J. 179
Bathrellou, E. 25
Bazzini, D. G. 27
Becker, C. B. 27
Beersma, B. 133
Bégin, C. 30
Bishop, K. 183
Boepple, L. 29
Bojorquez, A. 25
Boutelle, K. 24
Brewis, A. 169
Britton, L. E. 27
Brown, B. 126, 128, 133
Brown, C. S. 171, 172
Browne, N. T. 26
Brownell, K. D. 25, 31, 169
Brun, I. 24

Cameron, L. 26
Carr, D. 169
Carriere, L. J. 30
Cawley, J. 30
Chabrol, H. 25
Chen, C. 25
Chou, W. Y. S. 28
Christel, D. A. 183, 184
Ciao, A. 170
Cohen, R. 29, 30
Collisson, B. 30
Côté, M. 30
Cramer, P. 26
Cruwys, T. 27
Cunningham, G. B. 181
Curtin, L. A. 27

Daly, M. 169
Daníelsdóttir, S. 26,170
Dhurandhar, E. J. 170
Diedrichs, P. C. 27
Donaghue, N. 180

Dores Cruz, T. D. 133
Dulloo, A. G. 176

Eastin, M. 25
Ebbeck, V. 181
Eisenberg, M. E. 25
Eisenberger, N. I. 22
Ellefsen, S. 176
Engeln, R. 27
Evans, M. 183

Ferreira, C. 25
Flint, S. W. 180
Forhan, M. 26

Gavin, J. 29
Ghaznavi, J. 29
Gillen, M. M. 24
Granberg, E. M. 169
Greenberg, B. S. 25
Grosser, T. 133
Gruys, K. 183

Hackett, L. J. 183
Harriger, J. A. 25
Harrison, C. 171, 175
Hayes, S. C. 38
Hebert, E. 179
Heuer, C. A. 26, 31
Hofschire, L. 25
Hong, J. S. 26
Howell, J. L. 30

Irwin, L. 29

Jankowski, G. 27
Joyner, K. 30

Kasten, G. 169
Keery, H. 24
Kidwell, V. 133
Kilpatrick, M. 179
Kim, J. 29
King, K. M. 26
Kitchens, J. 38
Klein, H. 25
Kluck, A. S. 25, 30
Kunath, S. 28
Kyle, T. K. 170

Labianca, G. J. 133
Lachlan, K. 25
Latner, J. D. 26
LeaShomb, A. 27
Lee, J. M. 26
Lefkowitz, E. S. 24
Leverington, C. T. 27
Levine, M. P. 24
Lewis, S. 25
Li, W. 181
Lieberman, M. D. 22
Livingston, J. 180
Luedicke, J. 26
Luedke, M. 25
Lupton, D. 28

Major, B. 169
Mann, T. 176
Marta-Simões, J. 25
Martinescu, E. 133
Martz, D. M. 27
Matalas, A. L. 25
Mills, J. S. 27
Montani, J. P. 176
Morey, Y. 29
Morgan, J. T. 26
Mudry, T. 24
Muttarak, R. 30

Neumark-Sztainer, D. 25
Newton-John, T. 29, 30
Nichter, M. 27

Niens, U. 171, 172
Nieper, A. S. 133
Noor, N. M. 171, 172

O'Brien, K. S. 26, 170
Olds, T. 25
Oliveira, S. 25

Panza, G. A. 180
Paxton, S. J. 25
Pescatello, L. S. 180
Peters, L. D. 184, 185
Pettigrew, S. 25
Pickett, A. C. 181
Pires, C. 25
Poppenk, J. 93
Porges, S. W. 21, 2
Prestin, A. 28
Prévot, A. 176
Prys, N. A. 26
Puhl, R. M. 25, 26, 31, 169, 180

Rall, D. N. 183
Randle, M. 25
Reale, S. 180
Roberts, M. 38
Robertson, N. 180
Robertson, S. 25
Robinson, E. 169
Rodgers, R. F. 25
Roost, A. 26
Rosenfeld, E. 30
Rudolph, C. W. 31
Rukavina, P. B. 181
Rusbasan, D. 30
Russell-Mayhew, S. 24

Salafia, E. H. B. 25
Salk, R. H. 27
Sandoz, E. K. 38
Schaefer, M. K. 25
Schermer, F. 24
Schutz, Y. 176
Serier, K. N. 25
Shannon, A. 27
Sheldon, A. M. 27
Shen, B. 181
Shiffman, K. S. 25
Slater, A. 29, 30
Smolak, L. 24
Sobal, J. 30
Steinwert, T. 26
Stephan, Y. 169
Strosahl, K. D. 38
Sun, H. 181
Sundfør, T. M. 176
Sutin, A. R. 169

Talbot, C. V. 29
Taylor, B. A. 180
Taylor, L. D. 29
Terracciano, A. 169
Testori, M. 133
Thomas, S. L. 25
Thompson, I. 26
Thompson, J. K. 24, 25, 29
Tiggemann, M. 29
Tomiyama, A. J. 169, 176
Törneke, N. 22
Tredoux, C. 171, 172
Tropp, L. R. 171, 172
Tseng, J. 93
Tylka, T. L. 29, 30
Tzoutzou, M. 25

Udo-In-yang, I. 26

Van Den Berg, P. 24
Van Steen, T. 29
Viecelli, A. K. 176
Vohora, R. 180

Wall, M. M. 25
Weller, M. D. 31
Wells, C. L. 31
Werchan, C. 27
Willer, F. 176
Williams, K. D. 22
Wilson, K. G. 38
Wood-Barcalow, N. L. 29

Yoo, J. H. 29

Zaccardo, M. 29